Praying through the Prophets

John Calvin

Copyright © 2019 Berenice Aguilera

All rights reserved. No part of this publication may be reproduced, stored in a retrieval system, or transmitted by any means – electronic, mechanical, photographic (photocopying), recording, or otherwise – without prior permission in writing from the author.

ISBN: 9781098989682

Praying through the Prophets

(The Complete Series)

by

John Calvin

*"Those persons
who know the deep peace of God,
the unfathomable peace
that passeth all understanding,
are always men and women of much prayer."*
R. A. Torrey

Table of Contents

INTRODUCTION 1

JEREMIAH 3

LAMENTATIONS 79

EZEKIEL 87

DANIEL 111

HOSEA 143

JOEL 161

AMOS 167

OBADIAH 177

JONAH 181

MICAH 187

NAHUM 197

HABAKKUK 203

ZEPHANIAH 211

HAGGAI 217

ZECHARIAH 221

MALACHI 239

INTRODUCTION

The Bible is full of wisdom. It deals with so many ordinary matters, and fills our lives with such hope and promise, that it seems the most obvious place to go when it comes to praying. Whether we go through times of joy, there is a praise to be found and modeled, or whether a time of sorrow; again there are passages that can guide our thoughts and prayers. No matter what the circumstance, wisdom is to be found.

When I came across these prayers of John Calvin in his commentaries, combining both scripture and prayer, I knew I didn't just want to use them for myself, but to share them with others.

It is my earnest desire that this compilation of Calvin's prayers will encourage you to grow in God's grace and knowledge, and that God might reveal more of His love toward you.

God bless you.

Berenice Aguilera

JEREMIAH

Jeremiah 1:6-7

Grant, Almighty God, that as thou hast not only provided for thine ancient Church, by choosing Jeremiah as thy servant, but hast also designed that the fruit of his labors should continue to our age, O grant that we may not be unthankful to thee, but that we may so avail ourselves of so great a benefit, that the fruit of it may appear in us to the glory of thy name; may we learn so entirely to devote ourselves to thy service, and each of us be so attentive to the work of his calling, that we may strive with united hearts to promote the honor of thy name, and also the kingdom of thine only begotten Son, until we finish our warfare, and come at length into that celestial rest, which has been obtained for us by the blood of thine only Son. Amen.

Jeremiah 1:8-12

Grant, Almighty God, that since thou art pleased kindly to invite us to thyself, and hast consecrated thy word for our salvation, - O grant that we may willingly, and from the heart, obey thee, and become so teachable, that what thou hast designed for our salvation may not turn to our perdition; but may that incorruptible seed by which thou dost regenerate us into a hope of the celestial life so drive its roots into our hearts, and bring forth fruit, that thy name may be glorified; and may we be so planted in the courts of thine house, that we may grow and flourish, and that fruit may appear through the whole course of our life, until we shall at length enjoy that blessed life which is laid up for us in heaven, through Christ our Lord. - Amen.

Jeremiah 1:13-17

Grant, Almighty God, that as thou hast been once pleased to fortify thy servant Jeremiah with the invincible power of thy Spirit, - O grant that his doctrine may at this day make us humble, and that we may learn willingly to submit to thee, and so to receive and even cordially to accept what thou offerest to us by thy servant - to sustain us by thine hand, and that we, relying on thy power and protection, may fight against the world and against Satan, while each of us, in his vocation, so recumbs on thy power, as not to hesitate, whenever necessary, to expose our very life to dangers: and may we manfully fight and persevere in our warfare to the end, until having finished our course we shall at length come to that blessed rest which is reserved for us in heaven, through Christ our Lord. - Amen.

Jeremiah 1:19 – 2:1-5

Grant, Almighty God, that as thou continuest at this day, both morning and evening, to invite us to thyself, and assiduously exhortest us to repent, and testifiest that thou art ready to be reconciled to us, provided we flee to thy mercy, - O grant, that we may not close our ears and reject this thy great kindness, but that remembering thy gratuitous election, the chief of all the favors thou hast been pleased to shew us, we may strive so to devote ourselves to thee, that thy name may be glorified through our whole life: and should it be that we at any time turn aside from thee, may we quickly return to the right way, and become submissive to thy holy admonitions, that it may thus appear that we have been so chosen by thee and called as to desire to continue in the hope of that salvation, to which thou invitest us, and which is prepared for us in heaven, through Christ our Lord. - Amen.

Jeremiah 2:6-11

Grant, Almighty God, that since thou hast made thyself known to us in so plain a manner, not only by thy law and prophets, but also by thine only - begotten Son, that the knowledge of thy truth ought to have already struck deep roots in us, - O grant, that we may continue firm and constant in thy holy vocation, and make continual progress in it, and ever hasten forward to the goal: and do thou so humble us under thy mighty hand, that we may know that we are paternally chastised by thee, and profit under thy discipline, until being at length purified from all our vices we shall come to enjoy that immortal life, which has been made known to us by Christ, when we shall be able fully to rejoice in thee. - Amen.

Jeremiah 2:12-19

Grant, Almighty God, that as thou hast hitherto shewn to us so many favors, since the time thou hast been pleased to adopt us as thy people, - O grant, that we may not forget so great a kindness, nor be led away by the allurements of Satan, nor seek for ourselves inventions, which may at length turn to our ruin; but that we may continue fixed in our obedience to thee, and daily call on thee, and drink of the fullness of thy bounty, and at the same time strive to serve thee from the heart, and to glorify thy name, and thus to prove that we are wholly devoted to thee, according to the great obligations under which thou hast laid us, when it had pleased thee to adopt us in thine only - begotten Son. - Amen.

Jeremiah 2; 20-24

Grant, Almighty God, that, as it pleased thee, when thou didst deliver us from the tyranny of Satan, to lay on our necks thy yoke: - O grant, that we may be influenced by the spirit of docility, and of obedience, and of meekness, and willingly submit ourselves to thee through the whole course of our life, so that thou mayest gather from us the fruit of thy redemption: and may we so renounce sin that we may devote ourselves to thy service, and become the servants of righteousness, until having finished the course of our warfare, we shall be gathered into that blessed rest. which has been obtained for us by the blood of thine only - begotten Son. - Amen.

Jeremiah 2:25-30

Grant, Almighty God, that since thou, in thy paternal kindness, daily invitest us to thyself, we may not harden ourselves against thy holy and salutary admonitions: and whenever thou chastisest us with scourges, may we not become obdurate against thee, but learn humbly to submit to thy word, and receive thy chastisement, and so profit by both, that we may not be exposed to the extreme judgment which thou denouncest on the obstinate; but may we, on the contrary, open a way for thy paternal goodness, so that thou mayest kindly deal with us, until thou receivest us into that blessed rest which has been prepared for us in heaven, through Jesus Christ our Lord. - Amen.

Jeremiah 2:31-35

Grant, Almighty God, that since we are loaded with so many vices, and provoke thee so often, yea, daily and in ways innumerable, - O grant, that we may not at last become hardened against thy godly admonitions, but be teachable and submissive and in time repent, lest our wantonness and hardness should constrain thee to put forth thy powerful hand against us; but as we have hitherto experienced thy patental kindness, so may we in future be made partakers of it, and thus become more and more accustomed to bear thy yoke, until having at length completed our warfare, we shall come to that blessed rest, which has been provided for us in heaven, through Christ our Lord. - Amen.

Jeremiah 2:36 - 3:3

Grant, Almighty God, that as thou hast been once pleased not only to adopt us as thy children, but also to unite us to thyself by the bond of marriage, and to give us a pledge of this sacred union in thine only -

begotten Son, - O grant, that we may continue in the faith of thy Gospel, and so honestly keep the pledge given to thee, that thou mayest also shew thyself to us as a Husband and as a Father, and that we may to the end find in thee that merciful kindness which is needful to retain us in the holy fear of thy name, until we shall at length enjoy fellowship with thee in thy celestial kingdom, through Christ our Lord. - Amen.

Jeremiah 3:4-11

Grant, Almighty God, that since thou hast deigned to adopt us as thy people, and to unite us to thyself in thine only - begotten Son, - O grant, that we may continue pure and chaste in our obedience to thy Gospel, and never turn aside to those corruptions which disunite that sacred bond of union, which has been confirmed between us by the blood of thy Son, but that we may so persevere in serving thee, that our whole life and all our actions may be evidences of that holy calling, by which is laid up for us the hope of eternal salvation, until we shall at length come into the possession of that kingdom which has been obtained for us by so great a price, and there enjoy the fruit of our faith, sincerity, and perseverance, through Christ our Lord. - Amen.

Jeremiah 3:12-18

Grant, Almighty God, that as thou at this day mercifully sparest us, when yet in various ways we provoke thy displeasure, - O grant, that we may not harden ourselves against thy chastisements, but that thy forbearance may lead us to repentance, and that also thy scourges may do us good, and that we may so truly turn to thee, that our whole life may testify that we are in our hearts changed; and may we also stimulate one another, that we may unite together in rendering obedience to thy word, and each of us strive to glorify thy name, through Christ Jesus our Lord. - Amen.

Jeremiah 3:19-25

Grant, Almighty God, that as we cease not, though favored with many blessings, to provoke thee by our misdeeds, as though we avowedly carried on war against thee, - O grant, that we being at length warned by those examples, by which thou invitest us to repentance, may restrain our depraved nature, and in due time repent, and so devote ourselves to thy service, that thy name through us may be glorified, and that we may strive to bring into the way of salvation those who seem to be now lost, so that thy mercy may extend far and wide, and that thus thy salvation, obtained through Christ thine only - begotten Son, may be known and embraced by all nations. - Amen.

Jeremiah 4:1-6

Grant, Almighty God, that as we cease not daily to alienate ourselves from thee by our sins, and as thou yet kindly exhortest us to repent, and promisest to be appeasable and propitious to us, - O grant, that we may not perversely go on in our sins, and be ungrateful to thee for thy great kindness; but that we may so return to thee, that our whole life may testify that our repentance has been unfeigned, and that we may so acquiesce in thee alone, that the depraved lusts of our flesh may not draw us here and there, but that we may continue fixed and immovable in our purpose, and so labor to obey thee through the whole course of our life, that we may at length partake of the fruit of our obedience in thy celestial kingdom, through Jesus Christ our Lord. - Amen.

Jeremiah 4:7-14

Grant, Almighty God, that since thou art pleased daily to invite us to repentance, and since our own conscience is a witness, how we have in various ways provoked thy vengeance, - O grant, that we may not remain obstinate in our sins, nor harden our minds by perverse delusions, but suffer ourselves to be subdued by thy word, and so offer ourselves to thee with a pure and sincere heart, that our whole life may be nothing else but a striving for that newness which thou requirest; so that, being consecrated to thee in mind and body, we may ever labor to glorify thy name, until we be made partakers of that glory, which has been obtained for us by the blood of thy only - begotten Son. - Amen.

Jeremiah 4:15-22

Grant, Almighty God, that since thou hast not only once kindled among us the light of celestial truth, but also invitest us daily to partake of the salvation which has been set before us, - O grant, that we may not close our eyes, nor render deaf our ears, nor harden ourselves in our sins, but that as thou ceasest not continually to call us to thyself, so we may earnestly strive to hasten to thee, and to persevere in the course of our holy calling, so that we may draw nearer daily to its end, until thou receivest us at length into that celestial kingdom, which has been obtained for us by the blood of thine only-begotten Son. - Amen.

Jeremiah 4:23-30

Grant, Almighty God, that though we are torpid in our vices, we may yet be attentive to these examples of thy wrath, by which thou designest to warn us, so that we may learn by the misery of others to fear thee: and may we be also attentive to those threatenings, by which thou drawest us to thee, as thou failest to allure us by thy kindness: and may we, in the meantime, feel assured that thou wilt ever be propitious and merciful to all miserable sinners, who will from the heart seek thee and sincerely and unfeignedly repent; so that we may contend with our vices, and with real effort strive to deliver ourselves from those snares of Satan which he ever spreads for us, in order that we may more freely devote ourselves altogether to thee, and take such delight in thy righteousness, that our object and aim through the whole course of our life may be to please thee, and to render our services approved in Christ Jesus our Lord. - Amen.

Jeremiah 4:31 – 5:3

Grant, Almighty God, that as the devil ceases not to soothe us by his allurements, so that we may become torpid and stupefied, - O grant, that thy word may so shine in our minds and hearts that we may not grow torpid in darkness; and do thou also so rouse us by thy Spirit, that we may attend to those warnings of thy prophets, by which thou wouldest bring us to the right way, that we may not perish; and may we so assiduously exercise repentance through the whole course of our life, that we may ever be displeased with ourselves on account of our sins; and may we judge ourselves daily, that we may turn away from us thy wrath, until having at length finished our warfare, which we have to carry on continually with our sins, we shall come to that blessed rest which has been procured for us in heaven, by Jesus Christ our Lord. - Amen.

Jeremiah 5:4-9

Grant, Almighty God, that as we are at this day inclined to those vices, to which we learn thine ancient people were too much given, - O grant, that we, being governed by thy Spirit, may not harden ourselves against those thy holy warnings, by which thou daily reprovest us and our sins, but that we may be teachable and obedient: and as we have hitherto too much resisted thee and carried on war with thy justice, may we learn to fight with ourselves and with our sins, and rely on thy word, until we gain the victory, and at length attain that triumph, which has been prepared for us in heaven by Jesus Christ our Lord. - Amen.

Jeremiah 5:10-15

Grant, Almighty God, that though thou mightest justly condemn us at this day for the gross and wicked impiety, which thou didst formerly condemn by the mouth of thy Prophet in thine ancient people, - O grant, that we may not proceed in our obstinacy, but learn with pliable minds, and in true docility of heart, to submit to thy word, so that it may not turn to our ruin, but that we may by experience find it to be appointed for our salvation, so that being inflamed with a desire for true religion, and also cleansed from the filth of depraved affections and of carnal lusts, we may devote ourselves wholly to thy service, until having put off the flesh and all its filth, we shall at length attain to that perfect purity, which is set before us in thy gospel, and be made partakers of thy eternal glory in Christ Jesus our Lord. - Amen.

Jeremiah 5:16-24

Grant, Almighty God, that since thou daily invitest us to thyself with so much kindness and benevolence, and since thy word continually sounds in our ears, - O grant, that we may not become deaf through the depravity of our flesh, but be attentive to hear the doctrine of salvation, and become so teachable and obedient, that we may be willing to be turned wherever thou pleasest, and to be guided in the way thou pointest out to us, until we shall at length reach that blessed rest, which has been prepared for us in heaven by Jesus Christ our Lord. - Amen.

Jeremiah 5:25-31

Grant, Almighty God, that since we have been hitherto extremely deaf to thy many exhortations, and also to those threatenings by which thou hast sharply stimulated us to repentance, - O grant, that this perverseness may not always remain in us, but that we may at length submit to thee, not only for a short time, but continually, so that we may to the end devote ourselves wholly to thee, and thus glorify thy name, that we may at last become partakers of that glory, which has been procured for us by the blood of thy only - begotten Son. - Amen.

Jeremiah 6:1-9

Grant, Almighty God, that since thou kindly invitest us to repentance, and urgest us also by setting before us examples of thy wrath, - O grant, that we may not continue perversely disobedient, but render ourselves tractable and submissive to thee, so that we may not meet with that dreadful severity which thou didst threaten to thine ancient people, but anticipate the wrath which thou didst formerly denounce on them; and may we thus with a pious heart return to thee, that we may find by experience that thou art ever a propitious Father to sinners, whenever with a sincere heart and without dissimulation they return to thee, through Christ Jesus our Lord. - Amen.

Jeremiah 6:10-15

Grant, Almighty God, that inasmuch as thou seekest daily to restore us to thyself, and so arrangest thy word, as now kindly to allure us, and then to reprove us severely, and even to drive us by threatenings, - O grant, that we may not be altogether unteachable; but so rule us by the spirit of meekness, that we may submit ourselves to thee and to thy holy word, and be so terrified by the fear of thy judgment as yet ever to taste of the sweetness of thy mercy, so that we may cleave to thee in Christ thy Son, until we shall at length fully know that thou art our Father, and enjoy the fruit of our adoption in the same Christ Jesus our Lord. - Amen.

Jeremiah 6:16-23

Grant, Almighty God, that as we cease not daily to give thee occasion of offense, and as thou ceasest not, in order to promote our salvation, to call us to the right way, - O grant, that we may be attentive to thy voice, and suffer ourselves to be reproved by it, and so submit ourselves to thee, that we may continually go on towards the mark to which thou invitest us, and that having at length finished our course in this life, we may enjoy the fruit of our obedience and faith, and possess that eternal inheritance which has been obtained for us by Jesus Christ our Lord. - Amen.

Jeremiah 6:24 – 7:4

Grant, Almighty God, that as we so abuse thy forbearance, that thou art constrained by our depravity to deal sharply with us, - O grant, that we may not be also hardened against thy chastisements, but may we with a submissive and tractable neck learn to take thy yoke, and be so obedient to thy government, that we may testify our repentance, not for one day only, and give no fallacious evidence, but that we may really prove through the whole course of our life the sincerity of our conversion to thee, b y regarding this as our main object, even to glorify thee in Christ Jesus our Lord. - Amen.

Jeremiah 7:5-11

Grant, Almighty God, that as thou buildest not at this day a temple among us of wood and stones, and as the fullness of thy Godhead dwells in thine only - begotten Son, and as he by his power fills the whole world, and dwells in the midst of us, and even in us, - O grant, that we may not profane his sanctuary by our vices and sins, but so strive to consecrate ourselves to thy service, that thy name through his name may be continually glorified, until we shall at length be received into that eternal inheritance, where will appear to us openly, and face to face, that glory which we now see in the truth contained in thy gospel. - Amen.

Jeremiah 7:12-19

Grant, Almighty God, that as we are inclined not only to superstitions, but also to many vices, we may be restrained by thy word, and as thou art pleased daily to remind us of thy benefits, that thou mayest keep us in the practice of true religion, - O grant, that we may not be led astray by the delusions of Satan and by our own vanity, but continue firm and steady in our obedience to thee, and constantly proceed in the course of true piety, so that we may at length partake of its fruit in thy celestial kingdom, which has been obtained for us by the blood of thine only - begotten Son. - Amen.

Jeremiah 7:20-24

Grant, Almighty God, that as thou hast at this day so clearly revealed to us thy will that there can remain no pretense of ignorance, we may on that account submit to thee with a freer and more ready mind, and that we may not only incline our ears to thee, but also so attend to thee with all our hearts, that we may desire no other thing than to make our whole life approved by thee: and as we cannot but turn aside, through our obstinacy and wickedness, from the right way, do thou so enlighten us by the Spirit of wisdom and knowledge, that we may strive to embrace whatever thou hast been pleased to prescribe to us in thy word, so that when the course of this life shall be finished, we may at length reach the goal, and partake of the fruit of our obedience, and enjoy that eternal inheritance, which thine only - begotten Son has procured for us by his own blood. - Amen.

Jeremiah 7:25-30

Grant, Almighty God, that since thou so constantly invitest us, daily and even hourly, to thyself, we may not give thee occasion to complain, as of thy people of old, that we are deaf and thus neglect thy holy admonitions, but that we may be teachable and submissive to thee, and that, as thou risest early, we may also be ready to meet thee, and be obedient to thee, not only for one day, but persevere through life in the same course, until at length we shall reach that blessed rest, prepared for us in heaven by Jesus Christ our Lord. - Amen.

Jeremiah 7:31 – 8:3

Grant, Almighty God, that as thou terrifiest us daily with thy judgments, and as it is needful for our sloth to be stimulated, and for our corruption to be thus corrected, - O grant, that we may be moved by thy threatenings, and at the same time suffer ourselves to be kindly invited by thee, and make such progress in thy word, that, being terrified by threatenings, we may also readily and willingly obey whenever thou in a paternal manner callest us to thyself, and labor in every way to devote ourselves wholly to thee, by subduing the corrupt affections of our flesh, so that nothing may hinder us to be submissive to thy will, until we shall at length enjoy the rest of that eternal inheritance, which thou hast promised to us in Christ Jesus our Lord. - Amen.

Jeremiah 8:4-9

Grant, Almighty God, that since thou ceasest not daily to rouse us, as also our sloth requires continual warnings, - O grant, that we may not be unteachable, and that our perverseness may not hinder us to return immediately and willingly to thee, from whom we have, through our own fault, alienated ourselves: and may we not only feel some desire to repent, but persevere so constantly in the exercise of penitence, that through the whole course of our life we may contend with our lusts, until having at length subdued them all, we shall reach the goal which has been set before us, and enjoy in heaven that eternal inheritance, which has been procured for us by the blood of thine only - begotten Son. - Amen.

Jeremiah 8:10-18

Grant, Almighty God, that since we have been abundantly taught by ancient examples how insane they are who bend not under thy threatenings, and repent not in due time while thou invitest them to repentance, - O grant, that we may wholly give up ourselves to be disciplined by thee, and that we may not only bear with submissive minds to be chastised, but also learn by thy warnings to return without delay to thee, and that we may so remain in obedience to thee, that with unceasing perseverance we may fight under thy banner, until having at length finished our warfare, we shall enjoy that blessed rest which has been prepared for us by Christ our Lord. - Amen.

Jeremiah 8:19 – 9:2

Grant, Almighty God, that since thou hast been pleased that the prophetic writings should be preserved for our use, that they may continually excite us to repentance, and that since thou stiffest up daily those who urge us by their exhortations, and draw us, as it were by force, to repent, - O grant, that there may not be in us such perverseness as we see existed in thine ancient people; but that we may render ourselves teachable, and be so moved by thy threatenings, as to anticipate thy judgment, lest we, mistaking thy forbearance, should at length be visited with that dread, described to us by thy servant Jeremiah, but that we may, on the contrary, find thee to the end to be not only a reconcilable but also a most merciful Father, until we shall at last enjoy a fuller knowledge of thy goodness in thy celestial kingdom, through Jesus Christ our Lord. - Amen.

Jeremiah 9:3-9

Grant, Almighty God, that as we cease not by our sins to provoke thee more and more, we may at least be warned by thy threatenings and the words of thy prophets, and may not continue obstinate in evil nor pertinaciously resist thy will, but that we may on the contrary learn to anticipate thy judgment and thus receive thy corrections, so that our sins may be hated by us, and that we may become judges of ourselves, in order that we may obtain pardon, and that having obtained it we may not doubt ever to call on thee as our Father, until thou at length gatherest us unto that blessed inheritance, which has been procured for us by the blood of thine only Son. - Amen.

Jeremiah 9:10-15

Grant, Almighty God, that as thou hast not only testified what is right by the Law and the Prophets, in order that we may form our life in obedience to thy will, but hast also made more fully known to us by thy Gospel what is perfect righteousness, - O grant, that being ruled by thy Spirit, we may surrender ourselves altogether to thee, and so acquiesce in thy Word alone, that we may not deviate either to the right hand or to the left, but allow thee alone to be wise, and that acknowledging our folly and vanity, we may suffer ourselves to be taught by thy Word, so that we may really prove that we are truly obedient to thee, until having at length completed the course of this life, we shall reach that heavenly rest which has been obtained for us by the blood of thine only-begotten Son. - Amen.

Jeremiah 9:16-24

Grant, Almighty God, that since thou settest before our eyes so many evils and vices by which we have provoked thine anger against us, and yet givest us the hope of pardon if we repent, - O grant us a teachable spirit, that we may with becoming meekness attend to thy threatenings, and be in such a way territlcd by them as not yet to despair of the mercy offered to us, but seek it through thy Son: and as he has once for all pacified thee by shedding his blood, so cleanse thou us also by thy Spirit from all our pollutions, until we at length stand immaculate before thee in that day when Christ shall appear for the salvation of all his people. - Amen.

Jeremiah 9:25-26

Grant, Almighty God, that as thou hast revealed to us in thy Gospel how guilty and miserable we are, we may learn to loathe ourselves, ard so He down confounded and despairing on account of the sins and guilt we have contracted, as yet to know that true glory is offered to us, and that we can be made partakers of it, if by true faith we embrace thy only-begotten Son, in whom is offered to us perfect righteousness and salvation: And grant also that we may so cleave to Christ, and so receive by faith his blessings, that we may be able, not only before the world, but also against Satan and death itself, to glory in thee, that thou alone art just and wise and strong; and may thy strength and justice and wisdom shine forth upon us in our iniquity and ignorance and infirmity, until we shall at length reach that ruiness of glory, which has been prepared for us in heaven by Christ our Lord. - Amen.

Jeremiah 10:1-6

Grant, Almighty God, that since thou hast made heaven and earth for our sake, and hast testified by thy servant Moses, that the sun, as well as the moon, to which foolish heathens ascribe divinity, are to be serviceable to us, and that we are to use them as though they were our servants, - O grant that we may, by thy so many blessings, have our minds raised upwards and contemplate thy true glory, so that we may faithfully worship thee only, and surrender ourselves so entirely to thee, that while we enjoy the benefits derived from all the stars, and also from the earth, we may know that we are bound to thee by so many favors, in order that we may be more and more roused to attend to what is just and right, and thus endeavor to glorify on earth thy name, that we may at length enjoy that blessed glory which has been provided for us by Christ our Lord. - Amen.

Jeremiah 10:7-11

Grant, Almighty God, that since thou hast exhibited thy glory to be seen by us, not only in the heavens and the earth, but also ill the law, in the Prophets, and in the Gospel, and hast so plainly made thyself known to us in thine only - begotten Son, that ignorance can be no excuse, - O grant that we may make progress in this knowledge by which thou kindly invitest to thyself, and may so constantly cleave to thee, that none of the errors of the world may draw us aside; but may we stand firm in thy word, which cannot deceive us, until we shall at length come to that celestial blessedness, when we shall enjoy thee face to face in thy glory, having been made fully conformable to thine image in Christ Jesus our Lord. - Amen.

Jeremiah 10:12-16

Grant, Almighty God, that as thou hast been pleased to shew thyself so plainly to us, and as thou art pleased to confirm us in thy truth, - O grant that we may not turn aside either to the right hand or to the left, but depend entirely on thy word, and so cleave to thee that no errors of the world may draw us aside: may we constantly persevere in that faith which we have learnt from thy Law and thy Prophets, and especially from thy gospel, where thou hast made thyself more clearly known to us, through Christ Jesus, until we shall at length enjoy thy full and perfect glory, when we shall be transformed into it in that inheritance, which has been purchased for us by the blood of thy only-begotten Son. - Amen.

Jeremiah 10:17-23

Grant, Almighty God, that as we are in like manner at this day so torpid, that we are not moved by thy threatenings, nor do the kind and friendly warnings, by which thou invitest us to thyself, prevail with us, - O grant that we may at length learn to attend to the truth, in whatever form thou settest it before us, and that we may be teachable and obedient, when thou only invitest us, and that if we become hardened, we may be also touched by thy threatenings, and not tempt thy patience, but suffer ourselves to be brought under thy yoke, and so submit to thee, that thou mayest through our whole life rule over us, and shew to us thy paternal love, so that, after having faithfully served thee in this world, we may come at length into that blessed rest which is prepared for us in heaven by Christ our Lord. - Amen.

Jeremiah 10:24-25

Grant, Almighty God, that since we are so torpid in our sins, except thou rousest us, that we profit not by the severe warnings by which thou didst formerly stimulate thine ancient people, and since we have also been already warned by many signs of thy wrath to seek repentance with increasing assiduity, - O grant that we may earnestly persevere in this course, and so submit to thee, that with patient and calm minds we may bear thy corrections: and may we in the meantime be fully assured that thou wilt ever be our Father, and never hesitate, even in death itself, to flee to thy mercy, until thou pourest forth thy wrath on the ungodly and the profane despisers of thy name, and shewest such compassion towards us, that we may know that thou hast not in vain promised that thy chastisements would ever be kind and paternal, in visiting the sins of those who hope in thee, through Christ our Lord. - Amen.

Jeremiah 11:1-8

Grant, Almighty God, that since thou hast been pleased daily to invite us to thyself with so ranch benignity and kindness, we may not with deaf ears turn aside from the doctrine which is set forth for our salvation, but that we may attend to it and persevere also in that obedience which thou justly requirest from us, so that we may make increasing progress in true religion, and so form the whole course of our life according to thy righteous law, that we may fight as good soldiers to thee in this world, until we shall at length come to that blessed rest, which is prepared for us in heaven, through Christ our Lord. - Amen.

Jeremiah 11:9-12

Grant, Almighty God, that since thou hast been pleased, in so kind a manner, according to thy paternal kindness, to invite us to thyself, we may not be refractory, but winingly and quietly submit ourselves to thee, and not wait until thou shakest us with terror, and shewest us signs of thy wrath; hut may we anticipate thy dreadful judgment, and thus always go on, so as to have no other object in view but to glorify thy name through the whole course of our life, until we shall at length be made partakers of that glory which thine only begotten Son has obtained for us. - Amen.

Jeremiah 11:13-17

Grant, Almighty God, that as thou hast deigned to gather us into thy Church, we may never turn aside in the least from the purity of thy worship, but always regard what pleases thee, and learn to direct our doings and our thoughts in obedience to thy truth, and worship thee so purely both in spirit and in external forms, that thy name may be glorified by us, and that we may especially retain that purity which thou everywhere commendest to us, so that we may be indeed the members of thy only begotten Son; and that as he has sanctified himself on our account, we may also through his Spirit be made partakers of the same sanctification, until he at length will gather us into his celestial kingdom, which he has obtained for us by his own blood. - Amen.

Jeremiah 11:18-23

Grant, Almighty God, that as thou remindest us in thy word of our many vices and sins, we may learn to direct our eyes and thoughts to thee, and never think that we have to do with a mortal being, but that we may anticipate thy judgment: and may we learn so to examine all our thoughts and try our feelings, that no hypocrisy may deceive us, and that we may not sleep in our sins; but that being really and truly awakened, we may humble ourselves before thee, and so seek thy pardon, that when we he down in true repentance, thou mayest absolve us in thy mercy, through the virtue of that sacrifice by which thine only - begotten Son has once for all reconciled us to thee. - Amen.

Jeremiah 12:1-4

Grant, Almighty God, that though the same hardness is inbred in us as in thine ancient people, we may not become rooted in it; but do thou rouse us by thy Spirit, that we may suffer ourselves to be gently governed by thyi word, and be so touched by thy threatenings, that we may not defer the time whenever thou an - nouncest to us thy judgment, but strive to be immediately reconciled to thee: and as there is no other way of being reconciled except through thine only -

begotten Son, may we in true faith embrace the favor which thou offerest to us in thy gospel, and also devote ourselves wholly to thee, being truly penitent of our sins; and as we ought to make progress to the end of life, may we strive more and more to put off all the lusts of our flesh, until we shall at length be made partakers of that glory which thine only - begotten Son has prepared for us. - Amen.

Jeremiah 12:5-10

Grant, Almighty God, that as thou hast not only been pleased to offer thyself to be our Shepherd, but hast also set over us thine only - begotten Son, that he might gather us into his own fold, and as he sweetly invites us daily by his voice to continue collected under his power and government, - O grant that we may suffer ourselves to be governed by him, and never be like wild and untameable beasts, but so obey his voice, that wherever he may call us we may be ready to follow, and thus proceed through the whole course of our life, until we shall at length reach the goal which is set before us, and be thence led to the fruition of that eternal inheritance and glory which thine only - begotten Son has obtained for us by his own blood. - Amen.

Jeremiah 12:11-15

Grant, Almighty God, that as at this day such a dreadful scattering terrifies us on every side, we may learn to raise up our eyes above the world and to hope for that which is now hidden from us, even that in executing thy judgments on the Church as well as on aliens, thou wilt be so merciful to the whole world, as that we may be gathered into the unity of faith: and may we labor to devote ourselves wholly to thy service and cultivate brotherly concord among ourselves: until we shall at length enjoy that eternal inheritance, which has been obtained for us by the blood of thine only - begotten Son. - Amen.

Jeremiah 12:16 – 13:9

Grant, Almighty God, that as so many of the people who have been gathered by thee, that they might be the body of thine only-begotten Son, have fallen away, and have by their ingratitude alienated themselves from the hope of eternal salvation, - O grant, that they may again at this day be united together, and hold with us the true unity of faith, so that with one heart and one mouth we may profess thee as our God and Father, and so learn to swear by thy name, that we may acknowledge thee as our Judge, and ascribe to thee all power over us, until we shall at length enjoy that eternal inheritance, into the hope of which thou hast called us and daily invitest; us, through Christ Jesus our Lord. - Amen.

Jeremiah 13:10-15

Grant, Almighty God, that as we are by nature frail vessels, and our frailty is such that we of ourselves melt away, and when we become stronger we cannot stand by our own power, - O grant, that being supported by thy power, we may indeed rejoice in the perpetuity of our salvation, not indeed relying on any earthly protection, but because thou hast been pleased to choose us as thy people: and may we at the same time so pursue the course of our life, that we may not by our perfidy exclude thy grace from us, but give place to thee, that we may be more and more enriched by those gifts which pertain to the hope of a future life, until we shall at length come to that full and perfect happiness, in thy celestial kingdom, which is laid up for us by Christ our Lord. - Amen.

Jeremiah 13:16-21

Grant, Almighty God, that as we are so slothful to hear thee, yea, inasmuch as our minds are taken up with so many vanities so that we deceive ourselves, - O grant, that thy Holy Spirit may so illuminate us, that we may not despise thy threatenings, but may learn to anticipate in time thy judgment, and thus obtain pardon; that being mindful of thy mercy, we may pursue the course of our calling, until we shall at length be received into that blessed rest, which has been obtained for us by thy only-begotten Son. - Amen.

Jeremiah 13:22-27

Grant, Almighty God, that as we are so slothful to hear thee, yea, inasmuch as our minds are taken up with so many vanities so that we deceive ourselves, - O grant, that thy Holy Spirit may so illuminate us, that we may not despise thy threatenings, but may learn to anticipate in time thy judgment, and thus obtain pardon; that being mindful of thy mercy, we may pursue the course of our calling, until we shall at length be received into that blessed rest, which has been obtained for us by thy only-begotten Son. - Amen.

Jeremiah 14:1-9

Grant, Almighty God, that since we are taught by the Teacher whom thou hast set over us, to seek our daily bread from thee, we may know that whenever thou chastisest us with scarcity, we are justly visited by thy hand; and shouldest thou at any time deal severely with us, may we never cease to implore thy mercy, and feel assured that thou wilt ever be merciful and propitious to us, provided we decline not from the way which thou hast pointed out to us, even that thy Son will reconcile us to thee, and that his blood is our only satisfaction; and may we not look to anything else, even in seeing our salvation, but that thy name may be more and more glorified through Jesus Christ our Lord. - Amen.

Jeremiah 14:10-14

Grant, Almighty God, that as thou dealest so kindly with us as daily to shew to us our sins and to exhort us to repent, and teachest us that thou art ready to give us forgiveness, - O grant, that we may not be of a refractory mind, nor flee away from thee, while thou so kindly invitest us to thyself, but learn seasonably to repent, and be touched with the fear of thy judgment, so that we may truly and from the heart seek that reconciliation, which has been procured for us by the blood of thine only - begotten Son; and as we can bring nothing of our own, may we submissively humble ourselves before thee, and also by faith embrace the gift of thine only - begotten Son. - Amen.

Jeremiah 14:15-20

Grant, Almighty God, that though we have been once reconciled to thee, and reconciliation has been testified to us in thy gospel, we yet cease not daily to provoke thy wrath, - O grant, that we may at least groan, and undissemblingly so condemn our vices, that we may be touched with real and deep sorrow, and thus learn to flee, not only once in our life, but every moment, to thy mercy, that thou mayest be reconciled to us, and not deal with us according to our merits; but since thou hast been once pleased to embrace us with paternal love, for the sake of thy only - begotten Son, continue this favor to us, until having at length been cleansed from all filth and pollution, we shall become partakers of thy celestial glory, through Christ our Lord. - Amen.

Jeremiah 14:21 – 15:2

Grant, Almighty God, that since thou art graciously pleased to exhort us to repent, and withholdest thine hand, yea, and allowest us the opportunity to repent, - O grant, that we may not obstinately provoke against ourselves thy extreme vengeance, but render ourselves obedient to thee, so that thou mayest not only hear others praying for us, but that our own prayers may also obtain pardon from thee, espedally through the intercession of Christ, thine only - begotten Son, who has once for all reconciled thee to us, and whose perpetual intercession is to continue to reconcile us to thee, until we shall appear at length before thee with all our spots and filth wholly washed away, and be made partakers of that glory which has been obtained for us by Christ our Lord. - Amen.

Jeremiah 15:3-9

Grant, Almighty God, that we may not by our hardness so provoke thy judgment against us, but may we through a meek and submissive spirit be so influenced by thy threatenings as to anticipate that vengeance, by which we see that all the reprobate and the perverse have been visited; and may we so endeavor by true repentance to obtain thy favor, that we may receive thy daily blessings and benefits, until we shall at length come to the full and real enjoyment of all those blessings, which have been laid up for us in thy celestial kingdom, through Christ, our Lord. - Amen.

Jeremiah 15:10-15

Grant, Almighty God, that as we cease not by our sins daily to provoke thy wrath against us, and are also ungrateful to thee and disobedient to thy heavenly doctrine, - O grant that we may at length know what we have hitherto deserved, and become so displeased with our vices, that being really and from the heart turned to thee, we may above all things seek to be reconciled to thee and received into favor, so that thou mayest rule us by thy Holy Spirit, and confirm us in true obedience and godliness, until we shall at length enjoy that eternal felicity which has been prepared for us in heaven by Christ our Lord. - Amen.

Jeremiah 15:16-19

Grant, Almighty God, that since thou hast at this day plainly made known to us thy will through the gospel of thy Son, so that we may by an unshaken faith embrace what is therein set forth to us, - O grant, that we may learn to be satisfied with thee alone, and to aequiesce in thy truth, and to renounce the whole world, so that we may never be moved by any threats and terrors, nor vacinate when the ungodly seem so proudly disposed to withdraw confidence in thee; but may we render to thee all due honor, so as not only to obey thee but also to perform the offices committed to us, and never to hesitate so to provoke the whole world against us, that howsoever hard our warfare may be we may firmly persevere in the course of thy holy calling, and may thus at length enjoy that triumph, which Christ thy only-begotten Son hath procured for us. - Amen.

Jeremiah 15:20 – 16:4

Grant, Almighty God, that as thou anticipatest us by thy word, so that we may not experience thy eternal severity, - O grant, that we may become teachable, and be so displeased with our vices, that we may not provoke more and more thy vengeance, but hasten to seek reconciliation with thee, and that relying on the Mediator whom thou hast given us, we may flee to thy mercy, until having been cleansed from all our filth, we shall at length be received into thy celestial kingdom, and there appear before thee in that parity from which we are as yet very distant, and shall enjoy that glory which thine only-begotten Son has obtained for us by his own blood. - Amen.

Jeremiah 16:5-13

Grant, Almighty God, that as we in various ways daily provoke thy wrath against us, and thou ceasest not to exhort us to repent, - O grant, that we may be pliant and obedient and not despise thy kind invitations, while thou settest before us the hope of thy mercy, nor make light of thy threatenings; but that we may so profit by thy word as to endeavor to anticipate thy judgments; and may we also, being allured by the sweetness of thy grace, consecrate ourselves wholly to thee, that thus thy wrath may be turned away from us, and that we may become receivers of that grace which thou offerest to all who truly and from the heart repent, and who desire to have thee propitious to them in Christ Jesus our Lord. - Amen.

Jeremiah 16:14-18

Grant, Almighty God, that as thou hast not given to thy servants a small corner only of the earth to dwell in, but hast designed to extend thy kingdom to the utmost borders of the earth, and to dwell with us, wherever we be, by thine only-begotten Son, - O grant, that we may offer ourselves as sacrifices to thee, and labor also so to regulate our life according to thy word that thy name may be glorified in and by us, till we shall become at length partakers of that celestial and eternal glory, which has been provided for us by Christ our Lord - Amen.

Jeremiah 16:19 – 17:4

Grant, Almighty God, that as thou kindly invitest us every day to repentance, and shewest thyself ready to be reconciled, - O grant that we may not through our perverseness reject so inestimable a favor, but submit ourselves to thee, and become so displeased with our vices as to be touched with a true and sincere concern for religion, and to labor through the whole course of our life for nothing else but to render ourselves and our duties approved by thee, and thus to glorify thy name, so that we may become at last partakers of that celestial and eternal glory which thine only-begotten Son has attained for us. - Amen.

Jeremiah 17:5-10

Grant, Almighty God, that as we are wholly nothing and less than nothing, we may know our nothingness, and having cast away all confidence in the world as well as in ourselves, we may learn to flee to thee as suppliants, and so put our trust in thee for our present life and for eternal salvation, that thou alone mayest be glorified: and may we be devoted to thee through the whole course of our life, and so persevere in humility and in calling on thy name, that thou mayest not only for once bring us help, but that we may know that thou art always present with those who truly and from the heart call upon thee, until we shall at length be filled with the fullness of all those blessings, which are laid up for us in heaven by Christ our Lord - Amen.

Jeremiah 17:11-14

Grant, Almighty God, that we may learn, whether in want or in abundance, so to submit ourselves to thee, that it may be our only and perfect felicity to depend on thee and to rest in that salvation, the experience of which thou hast already given us, until we shall reach that eternal rest, where we shall enjoy it in all its fullness, when made partakers of that glory, which has been procured for us by the blood of thine only-begotten Son. -Amen.

Jeremiah 17:15-21

Grant, Almighty God, that as thou hast not only in former times sent thy prophets, but makest the testimony of thy will to be declared to us daily, - O grant, that we may learn to render ourselves teachable and submissive to thee, and so willingly bear thy yoke, that thy holy word may gain among us that reverence which it deserves: and may we so submit ourselves to thee, while thou speakest to us by men, that we may at length enjoy a view of thy glory, in which will consist our perfect felicity; and that we may not only contemplate thy glory face to face, but also hear thee thyself speaking, and so speaking, that we shall delight in that sweetness, which is laid up for us in hope, through Christ, our Lord. - Amen.

Jeremiah 17:22-27

Grant, Almighty God, that as thou dost not now prescribe to us one day on which we are to testify that we are sanctified by thee, but commandest us to observe a sacred rest through our whole life, so as to renounce ourselves and the world, - O grant, that we may really contemplate this rest, and so crucify the old man, that being effectually united to thine only-begotten Son, we may become also partakers of that resurrection in which he has led the way, and be gathered into that celestial kingdom which he has procured for us by his death and resurrection, after having so fought in this world, under thy banner, that thou mayest ever reign in us and rule and govern us by thy Spirit, so that nothing throughout life may be our own doing, but that we suffer ourselves to be governed by thee, until thou at length become to us all in all. - Amen.

Jeremiah 18:1-12

Grant, Almighty God, that since we stand or fall at thy will, we may be conscious of our weakness and frailty, and constantly remember that not only our life is a shadow, but that we are wholly nothing, and thus learn to trust in thee alone, and to depend on thee alone and on thy good pleasure; and as it is thine to begin and to complete whatever belongs to our salvation, may we in real fear and trembling submit ourselves to thee, ever calling on thee, and casting all our cares into thy bosom, until being at length freed from all dangers, we shall be gathered into that eternal and blessed rest which has been obtained for us by' the blood of thine only-begotten Son. - Amen.

Jeremiah 18:13-17

Grant, Almighty God, that we may in due time anticipate thy wrath, and never so kindle it by our perverseness as to preclude every remedy; and then also when thou for a time chastisest us, do not wholly cast us away, but let this resort ever remain to us, to seek thee in the day of calamity and to find thee accessible, so that being reunited to thee we may find that thou rememberest mercy even in wrath, until we shall enjoy a full and real participation of thy favor and paternal love in thy celestial kingdom, which has been procured for us by the blood of thine only-begotten Son. - Amen.

Jeremiah 18:18-23

Grant, Almighty God, that since thou exhortest us daily, and even constantly to repent, by the doctrine of thy Gospel, and shewest thyself to us reconcilable, - O grant, that we may not disregard so incomparable a benefit, but with resigned minds devote ourselves wholly to thee, and that we may not so far provoke thy wrath as to be altogether reiected by thee, and to find at last that there is no mercy for us; but may we anticipate extreme judgment, while the time of thy good-will continues, and thus embrace the benefit of reconciliation which thou offerest to us, so that being thankful to thee and accepted in thine only-begotten Son, we may proceed in the course of our vocation, until we shall at length enjoy that eternal inheritance which thine only-begotten Son has obtained for us by his own blood. - Amen.

Jeremiah 19:1-5

Grant, Almighty God, that since thou hast been pleased to shew to us the way in which we cannot err, provided we obey thee, - O grant, that we may render ourselves really teachable and ready to obey, and never undertake anything but what we know is approved by thee, nor turn aside on the right hand or on the left; but continue in that form of worship which thou hast prescribed to us in thy word, so that we may be able to bear witness, not only before the world, but before thee and the holy angels, that we obediently follow thee; and may we never blend anything of our own, but with submissive minds worship thee alone, and strive to render ourselves wholly subject to thee, until having at length rendered to thee due service through the whole course of our life, we shall reach that blessed rest which thy Son has procured for us by his own blood. - Amen.

Jeremiah 19:6-15

Grant, Almighty God, that since thou hast been pleased to prescribe a rule for us, by which we may truly and purely worship thee, - O grant, that we may follow this plain rule, and never indulge our own imaginations, nor trifle with thee through our own fancies or through the foolish wisdom of our flesh, but continue in thy law, and in the doctrine which thine only-begotten Son, our Lord, has delivered to us, so that we may advance more and more in the knowledge of that glory, the foretaste of which thou givest us now, until we shall at length fully and perfectly enjoy it, when we shall be gathered into that celestial kingdom, which thy Son has procured for us by his own blood. - Amen.

Jeremiah 20:1-5

Grant, Almighty God, that we may not by our perverseness increasingly provoke thy wrath, but that whenever thou threatenest us, we may immediately fear and tremble at thy word, and also obey thee in the true spirit of meekness, and so dread thy threatenings as to anticipate thy judgment by true repentance, and thus strive to glorify thy name, that thou mayest become our strength and glory, and that we may be able not only before the world, but before thee and thy angels, really to glory, that we are that peculiar people whom thou hast favored with thy adoption, that thou mayest to the end carry on in us the work of thy grace, through Jesus Christ our Lord. - Amen.

Jeremiah 20:6-9

Grant, Almighty God, that as at this day a greater and viler impiety breaks forth than at any age, and thy sacred truth is treated with derision by many of Satan's drudges, - O grant, that we may nevertheless constantly persevere in it, nor hesitate to oppose the fury of all the ungodly, and relying on the power of thy Spirit, contend with them until that truth, which thou didst once proclaim by thy Prophets, and at length by thine only-begotten Son, and which was sealed by his blood, may attain its full authority, that as it proves to many the savor of eternal death, so it may also be a pledge to us of eternal salvation, until we shall be gathered into thy kingdom at the coming of the same thy Son Jesus Christ. - Amen.

Jeremiah 20:10-16

Grant, Almighty God, that as virulent tongues now surround us, and the devil has many mercenaries, who have nothing else in view but to prevent by clamors whatever is rightly derived from thee, and has proceeded from thy mouth, - O grant, that we may firmly oppose such intrigues, and also stand with resolute minds against all their violent artifices, and proceed in the course of thy holy calling, until we shall at length surely know that they who trust in thee, and faithfully devote themselves to thy service, are never left without thy help; and that, having at last finished our warfare, we may be gathered into that blessed rest which has been obtained for us by the blood of thine only-begotten Son. - Amen.

Jeremiah 20:17 21:5

Grant, Almighty God, that as we cease not to provoke thy wrath, and are also so slow to repent, - O grant, that we may at least so profit under thy threatenings and the manifestations of thy judgment, that we may give up ourselves wholly to thee, and hope, also for thy favor which has been for a time hidden from us, until with resigned minds we shall be able confidently to call on thee, and so prove our constancy, that thy name may be glorified in us, so that we may also be glorified in thee through Jesus Christ our Lord. - Amen.

Jeremiah 21:6-12

Grant, Almighty God, that as we cease not, by new crimes, daily to kindle thy wrath, we may not proceed to obstinacy or contempt; and since it is good for us to be chastised by thine hand, grant that we may resignedly submit to thy scourges, and allow thee to act the part of a Father towards us, in restoring us to the right way, and never cease to hope in thee, even when thou seemest to be angry with us; but may our hope regard that issue which thou promisest, even that evils themselves shall be an aid to our salvation, until having gone through all the miseries of the present life, we shall come into that blessed rest which thine only-begotten Son has procured for us. - Amen.

Jeremiah 21:13 – 22:5

Grant, Almighty God, that as thou hast been pleased to erect the throne of thy Son among us, we may suffer ourselves to be ruled by him, and not falsely boast that we are his people, but really prove that we truly and from the heart confess him as our King, that he may also so defend us through the whole course of life against all the assaults of our enemies, that we, ever relying on thine aid, and possessing our souls in patience, may at length be translated into that blessed glory and rest, which he has purchased for us by his own blood: - Amen.

Jeremiah 22:6-13

Grant, Almighty God, that since thou continuest both by chastising us, and by kindly alluring us to thyself, to deal with us in such a way as to find out whether we are healable, - O grant, that we may not he hardened either against thy threatenings or thy promises, but follow in a teachable spirit what thou shewest is pleasing to thee, and make progress in holy living, and become daily more watchful and diligent, until we shall at length reach the goal which is set before us, and receive the reward of our faith in thy celestial kingdom, which has been obtained for us by the blood of thine only-begotten Son. - Amen.

Jeremiah 22:14-19

Grant, Almighty God, that as it has pleased thee to perpetuate the memory of the dreadful vengeance which thou hast executed on the descendants of David, so that we may learn by their evils carefully to walk before thee, - O grant, that the forgetfulness of this example may never possess us, but that we may assiduously meditate on what is set before us, in order that we may thus endeavor to advance and promote the glory of thy name through the whole course of our life, so that we may at length be made partakers of thy celestial glory, which thou hast prepared for us, and which thine only-begotten Son has obtained for us by his own blood. - Amen.

Jeremiah 22:20-27

Grant, Almighty God, that as thou promisest to us rest nowhere except in thy celestial kingdom, we may never suffer ourselves, while travelling on the earth, to be allured and driven here and there; but may we in the meantime call on thee with resigned minds, and thus carry on our warfare, that; how much soever thou mayest he pleased by various contests to try and prove us, we may still continue to be thy faithful soldiers, until we shall enjoy that rest which has been obtained for us by the blood of thine only-begotten Son. - Amen.

Jeremiah 22:28 – 23:4

Grant, Almighty God, that since thou didst formerly take such heavy vengeance on the impiety of thine ancient people, that thou didst not spare even kings, who were representatives of Christ, nor their counsellors, - O grant, that we at this day may continue in obedience to thy word, and not so kindle thy vengeance against us by our ingratitude, as to provoke thee to punish us with that sad and dreadful desolation which thou formerly didst not in vain denounce on thy people; but may thy Church become more and more fruitful, so that we may know that thou art really gracious to us; and may we thus in quietness give thee thanks, and suffer ourselves to be ruled by thee, even by the hand of thine only-begotten Son, until we shall be gathered from our scattering in this world into that eternal rest which he has obtained for us by his own blood. - Amen.

Jeremiah 23:5-6

Grant, Almighty God, that we, having been all slaves to sin and to iniquity, but regenerated by the Spirit of thy only-begotten Son, may truly and with sincere desire seek to serve and worship thee alone, and so consecrate ourselves to thee, that it may appear that we do not falsely profess the name of Christ, but that we are truly his members, being partakers of that new life which he brought us; and may we make such progress in it, that, having finished our course on earth, we may at length come to that fullness of life and happiness which has been procured for us by him, and which is laid up in heaven for us. - Amen.

Jeremiah 23:7-11

Grant, Almighty God, that as thou hast been pleased to set before us an example of every perfection in thine only-begotten Son, we may study to form ourselves in imitation of him, and so to follow not only what he has prescribed, but also what he really performed, that we may prove ourselves to be really his members, and thus confirm our adoption; and may we so proceed in the whole course of our life, that we may at length be gathered into that blessed rest which the same, thine only-begotten Son, hath obtained for us by his own blood. - Amen.

Jeremiah 23:12-19

Grant, Almighty God, that as we are ever inclined to be led away by ensnaring flatteries, and thus seek death and final ruin for ourselves, - O grant that we may learn to tremble at those denunciations announced by the prophets, by which thou shewest to us thy wrath, so that we may be roused to true repentance, and not harden ourselves through thy forbearance in what is evil, but pursue our heavenly course, until having at length put off all our vices, we shall be restored to that perfect form in which thy holy image fully shines forth, through Jesus Christ our Lord. - Amen.

Jeremiah 23:20-24

Grant, Almighty God, that as nothing necessary to be known for salvation is wanting in thy holy and celestial oracles, we may carefully and diligently study them, and so labor to make progress in the fear of thy name, in reliance on that grace which is offered to us in Christ, that we may derive real fruit from the reading and hearing of thy word; and may we also learn to turn everything to edification, so that thy name may be really glorified in us, and that we may through the whole course of our life make progress in faith and repentance, until we shall at length attain to that perfect holiness, to which thou daily invitest us, when we shall be wholly divested of all the filth of our flesh, and become fully renewed after the image of thy Son, our Lord. - Amen.

Jeremiah 23:25-28

Grant, Almighty God, that as thou art graciously pleased daily to set before us thy sure and certain will, we may open our eyes and ears, and raise all our thoughts to that which not only reveals to us what is right, but also confirms us in a sound mind, so that we may go on in the course of true religion, and never turn aside, whatever Satan and his ministers may devise against us, but that we may stand firm and persevere, until having finished our warfare, we shall, at length come unto that blessed rest which has been prepared for us in heaven by Jesus Christ our Lord. - Amen.

Jeremiah 23:29-35

Grant, Almighty God, that as nothing is better for us or more necessary for our chief happiness, than to depend on thy word, for that is a sure pledge of thy good will towards us, - O grant, that as thou hast favored us with so singular a benefit, which thou manifest to us daily, we may be attentive to hear thee and submit ourselves to thee in true fear, meekness, and humility, so that we may be prepared in the spirit of meekness to receive whatever proceeds from thee, and that thus thy word may not only be precious to us, but also sweet and delightful, until we shall enjoy the perfection of that life, which thine only-begotten Son has procured for us by his own blood. - Amen.

Jeremiah 23:36 – 24:2

Grant, Almighty God, that since thou delayest with so much forbearance the punishments which we have deserved, and daily draw on ourselves, - O grant, that we may not indulge ourselves, but carefully consider how often, and in how many different ways we have provoked thy wrath against us, that we may thus learn humbly to present ourselves to thee for pardon, and with true repentance so implore thy mercy, that we may from the heart desire wholly to submit ourselves to thee, that whether thou chastisest us, or, according to thine infinite goodness, forgivest us, our condition may be ever blessed, not by flattering ourselves in our torpitude, but by finding thee to be our kind and bountiful Father, being reconciled to us in thine only-begotten Son. - Amen.

Jeremiah 24:3-7

Grant, Almighty God, that as we are placed in this world, that while daily receiving so many blessings, we may so pass our time as to regard our end and hasten towards the goal, - O grant, that the benefits and blessings by which thou invitest us to thyself, may not be impediments to us, and keep us attached to this world, but on the contrary stimulate us to fear thy name as well as to appreciate thy mercy, so that we may thus know thee to be our God, and strive on our part to present ourselves to thee as thy people, and so consecrate ourselves and all our services to thee, that thy name may be glorified in us, through Christ our Lord. - Amen.

Jeremiah 24:8 – 25:5

Grant, Almighty God, that since thou hast been pleased to choose us from our infancy to be thy people, and that when we were wretched apostates, thou hast also been pleased to restore us to the right way, by stretching forth thine hand to lead us, - O grant, that we may not be deaf nor idle; but may it please thee, by thy Spirit, especially to correct all obstinacy in our hearts, so that we may render ourselves obedient and submissive to thee: and as thou hast not ceased continually to call us, may we in our turn respond to thee, and not only by our tongues, but also by our works, pursue the course which thou hast appointed for us, until we shall reach the goal, and enjoy that blessed state of glory which thou hast prepared for us in heaven, through Christ our Lord. - Amen.

Jeremiah 25:6-12

Grant, Almighty God, that as we see everywhere evidences of thy wrath, and as our own conscience convinces every one of us, so that we are constrained to confess that we are all, from the highest to the lowest, guilty before thee, - O grant that we may in due time return to the right way, and seek to be reconciled to thee, and never doubt but that thou wilt be merciful and gracious to us, whenever we solicit pardon in the name of thy only-begotten Son; and may we also be so reconciled to thee, that we may know that thou art indeed with us as our Father, by ruling us by thy Spirit, so that thy name may to the end be glorified, through our Lord Jesus Christ. - Amen.

Jeremiah 25:13-19

Grant, Almighty God, that as we cease not to abuse thy paternal kindness, that when thou sparest us for a time, it is made by us the occasion of more audacity and liberty in sin, - O grant that we may be so subdued by thy scourges as to return without delay to thee, and to seek reconciliation with thee through the blood of thine only-begotten Son, and also to be so displeased with our vices, that we may from the heart submit to thee, so as to be governed by thy Holy Spirit, until, having been cleansed from all our filth, we shall come to that blessed glory which thou hast prepared for us in heaven, and which has been obtained for us by the blood of the same, thy Son Jesus Christ. - Amen.

Jeremiah 25:20-27

Grant, Almighty God, that since there are before our eyes so many evidences of thy judgments and of thy goodness, we may advance in the fear of thy name, and not go on to kindle thy wrath more against us, but that, being touched with true repentance, we may seek to be reconciled to thee, and that, commiserating the many evils, by which the world is at this day afflicted, we may also strive to restore those to the right way who seem to give themselves up to their own ruin, so that by converting those to thee who are now far away and aliens, thy name may be more glorified and proclaimed by us with one consent, through Christ Jesus our Lord. - Amen.

Jeremiah 25:28-31

Grant, Almighty God, that as thou seekest continually in various ways to restore us to thyself, - O grant, that we may not by our untameable perverseness resist thy holy and kind admonitions, nor continue torpid in our drowsiness, but anxiously flee to thee, and so humbly solicit pardon, that we may thus shew that we really and habitually repent, so that thy name may in every way be glorified, until we shall come into thy celestial glory, through Christ Jesus our Lord. - Amen.

Jeremiah 25:32-38

Grant, Almighty God, that as thou hast been pleased to gather us, so that we may be under thy protection and care, and to offer thyself to be our Shepherd, and even to exhibit thyself as such through thine only-begotten Son, - O grant, that we may willingly obey thee and hearken to the voice of that Shepherd whom thou hast set over us, so that we may be preserved to the end by thy goodness and power, and never wander from thee nor be carried away by our lusts, but so continue under the shadow of thy wings, that thou mayest be ever present with us and check our enemies, so that we may remain safe under thy protection throughout life, as well as in death, through the same Christ Jesus our Lord. - Amen.

Jeremiah 26:1-6

Grant, Almighty God, that as thou hast been pleased not only to make known thy will once by the Law, but also to add more light by thy holy prophets, and further to give us perfect light by thy Gospel, and as thou invitest us daily to learn by means of those whom thou hast sent, - O grant, that we may not be deaf nor tardy to hear, but promptly submit ourselves to thee, and so suffer ourselves to be ruled by thy word, that through our whole life we may testify that thou art indeed our God, we being thy people, until we shall at length be gathered into that celestial kingdom, which thine only-begotten Son our Lord has purchased for us. - Amen.

Jeremiah 26:7-13

Grant, Almighty God, that since thou hast not only called us once to the hope of an eternal inheritance, but invitest us continually to repentance, while we cease not by our continual sins to depart from thee, - O grant that we may not with deaf ears reject thy voice, but be pliable and submissive to thee, and that we may also so accustom ourselves to bear the yoke, that we may prove, through our whole life, that we are of thy sheep, and that Christ, thine only-begotten Son, whom thou hast set over us, is indeed our Shepherd, until we shall be gathered unto that kingdom which he has obtained for us by his own blood. - Amen.

Jeremiah 26:14-19

Grant, Almighty God, that since thou hast been pleased to gather us as a people to thyself, and to promise that we should be like a spiritual temple for thee to dwell in, - O grant that we may consecrate among us a perpetual habitation for time, and so strive through the whole course of our life to devote ourselves to thee, that thy grace and blessing may never depart from us, but that we may experience more and more that those are never destitute of thy protection who truly and undissemblingly rely on thee, so that thy name may be more and more glorified in us through thine only-begotten Son. - Amen.

Jeremiah 26:20 – 27:5

Grant, Almighty God, that when at any time thou grievously threatenest us, we may not, on that account, become angry, but learn to acknowledge our sins, and truly to humble ourselves under thy mighty hand, and also to deprecate thy wrath, and to prove by true repentance, that we profit by thy word, and believe thy denunciations, so that we may become partakers of that mercy, through which thou promisest to be propitious to all who turn to thee: and may we thus advance more and more, and persevere in the right course of repentance, until having at length put off all the vices of the flesh, we shall attain to a perfection of righteousness and the fruition of that glory which has been laid up for us in heaven by Jesus Christ our Lord. - Amen.

Jeremiah 27:6-8

Grant, Almighty God, that as we cease not in various ways to arm thine hand against us, we may, being at least touched by thy holy admonitions, humble ourselves under thy mighty hand, and thus anticipate thy judgment, so that thou mayest meet us as a merciful and gracious God, and not only remit to us the punishments which we have deserved, but also shew and perpetuate to us thy paternal favor, until, having been led by thine hand, we shall come unto that celestial kingdom which thou hast prepared for us, and which has been obtained for us by the blood of thine only-begotten Son. - Amen.

Jeremiah 27:9-18

Grant, Almighty God, that as we cease not often and continually to provoke thy wrath against us, we may of our own accord anticipate thy judgment, and not harden ourselves in our sins, having been especially warned by thy word, but in due time repent, and so submit ourselves to thee, that whatever thou mayest appoint for us, we may not doubt but thou wilt be propitious to us; and while fleeing to thy mercy, may we not refuse the punishment thou deemest expedient to bring us to the right way, until having at length put off all our corruptions, we shall enjoy that eternal inheritance, which is laid up for us in heaven, through Jesus Christ our Lord. - Amen.

Jeremiah 27:19 – 28:6

Grant, Almighty God, that as thou continuest to invite us to thyself, and often to remind us of our sins, that we may embrace the hope of mercy that is offered to us, - O grant, that we may not be ungrateful for this so great and invaluable a blessing, but come to thee in real humility and true repentance, and that trusting in thine infinite goodness, we may not doubt but that thou wilt be propitious to us, so that we may be kindled with the desire for true religion, and in all things obey thy word, that thy name may be glorified in us, until we shall at length come into that celestial glory, which thy Son hath obtained for us by his blood. - Amen.

Jeremiah 28:7-11

Grant, Almighty God, that since thou wouldest so try the constancy of our faith as to permit the devil to blend his lies with thy holy truth, we may not yet be entangled in them, but be attentive to that light which thou settest before us, and by which thou guidest us into the way of salvation; and may we in the spirit of docility so offer ourselves to be ruled by thee, that thou mayest also become our faithful and infallible leader, until we shall at length attain that eternal life which has been obtained for us by the blood of thine only-begotten Son. - Amen.

Jeremiah 28:12-17

Grant, Almighty God, that as thou dost kindly and graciously invite us to repentance, we may be so touched by the sense of thy wrath, that we may not by our perverseness increase more and more the heinousness of thy vengeance against us, but lay hold on the mercy that is offered to us, so that we may experience the efficacy and fruit of thy truth for our salvation, through Christ our Lord. - Amen.

Jeremiah 29:1-7

Grant, Almighty God, that we may be more and more habituated to render obedience to thee, and that whenever thou chastisest us with thy scourges, we may examine our own consciences, and humbly and suppliantly deprecate thy wrath, and never doubt but thou wilt be propitious to us, after having chastised us with thy paternal hand; and may we thus recumb on thy fatherly kindness, that we may ever look forward with quiet minds, until the end appears, which thou hast promised to us, and that when the warfare of this present life shall be finished, we may reach that blessed rest, which has been prepared for us in heaven, through Christ our Lord. - Amen.

Jeremiah 29:8-11

Grant, Almighty God, that since thou hast been pleased kindly to shew to us thy paternal love, and givest us daily a testimony of it in thy Gospel, - O grant, that we may not go astray, following our vagrant and erring thoughts, but acquiesce in thy simple truth; and though we must be exercised in this world by many conflicts, as our life is to be as it were a continual warfare, may we yet never doubt but that there is prepared for us a sure rest in heaven through Christ our Lord. - Amen.

Jeremiah 29:12-19

Grant, Almighty God, that as thou hast given so remarkable a proof both of thy wrath and of thy paternal kindness in thy dealings with thine ancient people, - O grant, that we may not by our obstinacy provoke thine extreme wrath, but in time anticipate thy judgment, so that we may find thee reconcilable, and never doubt but that thou wilt be merciful to us when we sincerely turn to thee; and as we are so prone to all evil, yea, and rush headlong into it, and as our wickedness and hardness are so great, grant to us, we pray thee, the spirit of meekness, that we may in all things submit ourselves to thee, and thus render ourselves thy children, that we may also find thee to be our Father in thine only-begotten Son. - Amen.

Jeremiah 29:20-27

Grant, Almighty God, that since we are prone to what is false, and wholly devoted to vanity, we may be governed by thy Spirit, and desire no other thing than to be obedient to thee; and as we offer ourselves to thee, as thy disciples, grant that having the light of thy word shining before us, we may follow the way which thou shewest to us, and thus persevere in a right course, until we shall at length come to that blessed rest which is prepared for us in heaven, through Christ our Lord. - Amen.

Jeremiah 30:1-7

Grant, Almighty God, that as we cease not in various ways perversely to provoke thy wrath against us, - O grant that we may at length be turned to obedience by thy kind admonitions, and at the same time submit also to thy just severity, and know that whenever thou severely chastisest us, we are dealt with as we deserve: may we yet never despond, but flee to thy mercy, not doubting but that thou in the midst of wrath rememberest thy paternal love, provided we rely on that favor which thou hast promised to us through thine only-begotten Son. - Amen.

Jeremiah 30:8-11

Grant, Almighty God, that as we are born wholly alienated from thy kingdom and the hope of salvation, and as a dreadful scattering awaits us except thou gatherest us by the power and grace of thy Spirit, - O grant, that as thou hast once adopted us as thy people, and hast been pleased to gather us under the yoke of Christ, we may remain in obedience to him, and thus continue under thy government, that after having completed our course in this life, we may at length come unto that kingdom where we shall enjoy all those good things which we now only by hope taste, through the same, Christ Jesus our Lord. - Amen.

Jeremiah 30:12-18

Grant, Almighty God, that since we are so slow to consider thy judgments, and become continually hardened in our sins, - O grant, that being really touched by those many warnings by which thou not only invitest, but also stimulatest us to repent, we may learn to humble ourselves, and so Submit to thy chastisements, that we may be capable of receiving that mercy which turns whatever evil may happen to us to our good and salvation, until we shall at length be gathered into that blessed rest which is prepared for us in heaven, through Christ our Lord. - Amen.

Jeremiah 30:19-22

Grant, Almighty God, that as thou hast manifested to us in thine only-begotten Son all the paternal goodness of which the fathers formerly tasted, and hast so really and fully exhibited it, that nothing more can be desired by us, - O grant, that we may remain fixed in our trust in thee, and so cleave by true faith and in sincerity of heart to our Redeemer, that we may expect from him all things necessary for our salvation: and may we know that whatever may happen to us, we are still blessed, provided we enjoy this singular privilege, to call on thee as our Father through the name of the same thy Son. - Amen.

Jeremiah 30:23 – 31:5

Grant, Almighty God, that as thou hast once testified that thou art to us a Father through thine only-begotten Son, we may not only taste of that promise, but be also wholly satisfied with it, and remain in it constantly, until having gone through all evils, we may at length attain to the full manifestation of it, when thou gatherest us into that blessed rest, which is the fruit of thy eternal adoption, through the same Christ Jesus our Lord. - Amen.

Jeremiah 31:6-9

Grant, Almighty God, that as thou hast so often been pleased to receive into favor thine ancient people, though extremely provoked by their perverse wickedness, - O grant, that mercy may also at this day be shewn to us, and that though we wholly deserve to perish eternally, thou mayest yet stretch forth thine hand to us and grant to us a testimony of thy favor, so that we may be able with a cheerful mind to call on thee as our Father, and ever to entertain hope of thy mercy, until we shall be gathered into that kingdom, where we shall perfectly render to thee the sacrifice of praise, and rejoice in the fruition of that eternal life, which has been procured for us by the blood of thine only-begotten Son. - Amen.

Jeremiah 31:10-13

Grant, Almighty God, that as we are still in our state of pilgrimage, and as thou makest us partakers of thy goodness, according as thou knowest to be necessary for us, - O grant, that we, being ever reminded by thy benefits, may aspire to higher things, and may, through all the temptations with which we must contend, advance towards the goal set before us, looking for that perfect felicity in heaven, of which a few sparks only now shine before our eyes, and thus carry on a warfare under the banner of thy Son, so as not to doubt but that a triumph is prepared for us in that blessed life which has been obtained by his blood. - Amen.

Jeremiah 31:14-18

Grant, Almighty God, that as we are always carried away by our own vanities, and as the licentiousness and insolence of our flesh are such that we never follow thee and submit to thy will, - O grant, that we may profit more and more under thy scourges, and never perversely harden ourselves, but learn to know that even when thou appearest rigid, thou hast a regard for our salvation, so that we, turning to thee, may strive during the rest of our life to glorify thy name through thine only-begotten Son. - Amen.

Jeremiah 31:19-21

Grant, Almighty God, that as pertinacity is inbred in us, so that we always struggle against thee, and are never tractable until we are renewed by thy Spirit, - O grant, that thy chastisements by which thou wouldest restore us to a sound mind, may not prove ruinous to us, but so influence us by thy Spirit within, that we, being really humbled, may acknowledge thee as our Judge and Father - our Judge, in order that we may be displeased with ourselves, and being touched by thy judgment, we may condemn ourselves, - and our Father, in order that we may, notwithstanding, flee to that mercy which is daily offered to us in the Gospel, through Christ Jesus our Lord. - Amen.

Jeremiah 31:22-30

Grant, Almighty God, that since thou warnest us daily by so many evidences of thy wrath, that we may in due time repent, - O grant, that we may not be slow to consider thy work, and also the doctrine which thou addest, but anticipate thy extreme vengeance, and thus be made capable of receiving thy mercy, that as thou freely offerest it to us, we may anxiously embrace it, and also so retain it in our hearts by true faith, that thou mayest continue its course towards us, until we shall at length reach that blessed rest, which has been prepared for us in heaven by Christ our Lord. - Amen.

Jeremiah 31:31-34

Grant, Almighty God, that as thou hast favored us with so singular a benefit as to make through thy Son a covenant which has been ratified for our salvation, - O grant, that we may become partakers of it, and know that thou so speakest with us, that thou not only shewest by thy Word what is right, but speakest also to us inwardly by thy

Spirit, and thus renderest us teachable and obedient, that there may be an evidence of our adoption, and a proof that thou wilt govern and rule us, until we shall at length be really and fully united to thee through Christ our Lord. - Amen.

Jeremiah 31:35-36

Grant, Almighty God, that as we enjoy the light of the sun by day, and of the moon by night, we may learn to raise higher our eyes, and not be like the unbelieving, who have this benefit in common with us, but look forward in hope of our eternal salvation, nor doubt but that as thou settest before our eyes a proof of thy immovable constancy in these created things, so also secure and certain shall be our salvation, which is founded on thy most certain truth, which renders sure all things, until at length we come into that blessed kingdom, which has been obtained for us by the blood of thy only-begotten Son. - Amen.

Jeremiah 31:37 – 32:3

Grant, Almighty God, that since we cease not daily to provoke thy wrath against us, we may be warned by thy word and repent, and so humble ourselves before thee that we may anticipate the rigor of thy judgment, and that being also chastised by thy hand, we may not become hardened, but be submissive to thee and teachable, and so profit under thy discipline, that being at length wholly devoted to thee, we may have no other object than to glorify thy holy name, until we shall become partakers of that glory which thine only-begotten Son has obtained for us. - Amen.

Jeremiah 32:4-15

Grant, Almighty God, that since we have at this day the evidence of eternal salvation sealed in earthen vessels, and thou invitest us to the hope of that blessed inheritance by the voice of men, - O grant, that we may not judge of the permanence of thy faithfulness by the appearance of those whom thou hast made our ministers, but relying on thy perpetuity, may we never doubt but that that life will be kept safe for us, which now every moment seems to vanish away, until at last we shall come to the full fruition of it in Christ Jesus our Lord. - Amen.

Jeremiah 32:16-20

Grant, Almighty God, that as our whole wisdom is this, to submit ourselves to thee, to admire, and receive, and reverently to adore thy judgments, - O grant, that we may not indulge the perverse thoughts of our flesh, but so learn to check and restrain ourselves as ever to render to thee the praise due to thy wisdom, and justice, and power, and thus walk in sobriety of mind while we sojourn in this world, until we shall at length contemplate thy glory thee to face, being made partakers of it in Christ Jesus our Lord. - Amen.

Jeremiah 32:21-29

Grant, Almighty God, that as thou shewest that thou so rulest over the whole world as to exercise a peculiar care over us whom thou hast been pleased to gather into the bosom of thy Church, - O grant, that we may be so restrained by thy awful power within the bounds of our duty, as that we may yet be always fully persuaded that thou art our God and Father, and thus submit ourselves willingly to thy word, and not only taste of thy goodness, which is laid up for thy children, but also feed on it, so that we may at length come into thy blessed kingdom above, where there will be full satisfaction and fruition, through Jesus Christ our Lord. - Amen.

Jeremiah 32:30-34

Grant, Almighty God, that as thou stretchest forth thy hand to us daily, and invitest us also by continual exhortations to repentance, - O grant, that we may not be so ungrateful as by our obstinacy to reject such and so great a benefit; but that, if at any time we should happen to turn from the right way, we may immediately tuae to thee and become obedient to thy will, and that thus the medicine which thou hast provided for us may avail for our salvation, until, being at length purified from all vices, we shall enjoy that blessed and immortal glory which thou hast prepared for us in heaven, through thine only-begotten Son, our Lord. - Amen.

Jeremiah 32:35-39

Grant, Almighty God, that since our earthly life is appointed as a life of warfare, and we must necessarily be exposed to continual disquietude as long as we sojourn here, - O grant, that we may always look forward to that blessed rest, to which thou invitest us, and in the meantime remain quiet in dependence on thy protection, and courageously fight to the end, not doubting but that through thy favor all things shall turn out for good, until we shall at length enjoy that eternal and glorious inheritance, which is laid up for us in heaven, through Christ our Lord. - Amen

Jeremiah 32:40-41

Grant, Almighty God, that since we are by nature wholly addicted to evil and bring nothing from the womb but depravity, - O grant, that being regenerated by thy Spirit we may strive to please and obey thee; and as our frailty is such that we may at any moment fall away, simply thou us with firmness and constancy, that we may never faint in the middle of our course, but so constantly obey thee, that we may at length enjoy that blessed rest, which is prepared for us, after we shall have passed through our earthly warfare, in Christ Jesus our Lord. - Amen.

Jeremiah 32:42 – 33:6

Grant, Almighty God, that we may so learn to humble ourselves under thy mighty hand, whenever thou chastisest us, that we may not faint in our miseries, but flee to thy mercy with more confidence, and by acknowledging our sins, may become so displeased with ourselves, that we may never lose the taste of thy mercy but gird ourselves up so as to entertain good hope, and call upon thee, until we shall at length find by success that our prayers are not in vain; and may we ever thus find comfort in our evils, so that we may at length enjoy that perfect felicity, which thou hast prepared for us in heaven, through Christ our Lord. - Amen.

Jeremiah 33:7-11

Grant, Almighty God, that as we cease not to separate ourselves often from thee, we may at least know that reconciliation is prepared for us, provided we seek it by a true and sincere faith in thine only-begotten Son, and so return to thee as really to loathe ourselves on account of our sins, and that relying on thine infinite mercy we may never doubt but that thou wilt be reconciled to us, until having at length finished our present course of life, and being cleansed from all the pollutions of the flesh, we shall be clothed with that celestial glory, which thy Son by his death and resurrection has obtained for us. - Amen.

Jeremiah 33:12-16

Grant, Almighty God, that since thou hast been pleased to perform to the Jews what thou didst promise, by sending the Savior, and hast also designed, by pulling down the middle wall of partition, to make us partakers of the same invaluable blessing, - O grant, that we may embrace him with true faith, and constantly abide in him, and so know thee as our Father, that, being renewed by the Spirit of thy Son, we may wholly devote ourselves to thee, and consecrate ourselves to thy service, until at length that which is begun in us be completed, and we be filled with that glory to which thy Son, our Lord, daily invites us. - Amen.

Jeremiah 33:17-26

Grant, Almighty God, that as thou settest before us daily, both in the heavens and on the earth, an illustrious example, not only of thy power and wisdom, but also of thy goodness and faithfulness, - O grant, that we may learn to raise up our thoughts still higher, even to that hope which is laid up for us in heaven, and that we may so suffer ourselves to be agitated by the various changes of this world, that yet our hope may remain fixed in thee, and that whatever may happen, we may be fully persuaded that thou wilt be in such a way our Father, that we shall at length enjoy that blessed rest, which has been obtained for us by the blood of thine only-begotten Son. - Amen.

Jeremiah 34:1-5

Grant, Almighty God, that as it is ever expedient for us to be often chastised by thine hand, - O grant, that we may learn to bear thy scourges patiently, and with quiet minds, and so acknowledge our sins, that we may not at the same time doubt but that thou wilt be merciful to us, and that we may with this confidence ever flee to seek pardon, and that it may avail also to increase our repentance, so that we may strive more and more to put off all the vices of the flesh, and to put on the new man, so that thine image may be renewed in us, until we shall at length come to partake of that eternal glory, which thou hast prepared in heaven for us, through Christ thy Son. - Amen.

Jeremiah 34:6-15

Grant, Almighty God, that since we have been redeemed by thine only-begotten Son, not only from temporal servitude, but also from the miserable tyranny of the devil and death, - O grant, that we may acknowledge thee as our Deliverer, and so wholly devote ourselves to thee, that we may also labor to serve one another, and by mutual acts of kindness so cherish among ourselves brotherly love, that it may appear that thou indeed rulest among us, and that we are subject to thee through the same thy Son. - Amen.

Jeremiah 34:16-22

Grant, Almighty God, that as we cease not continually to provoke thy wrath against us, - O grant, that we, being terrified by thy warnings, may obey thy wise counsels, and that thus by anticipating thy vengeance, which would otherwise remain on us, we may labor to be so reconciled to thee, that we may really find thee to be our Father and the guardian of our salvation, until we shall at length, having finished our course here, come to that blessed rest, which thou hast prepared for us in heaven, through Christ our Lord. - Amen.

Jeremiah 35:1-7

Grant, Almighty God, that as thou hast been pleased to adopt us for thy children, and also to shew to us what pleases thee, - O grant, that we may in all things be obedient to thee, and never turn aside either to the right or to the left; and as thou exhortest us also continually, and stirrest us onward, grant that we may, in quiet meekness of spirit, so surrender ourselves to be ruled by thee, as to prove ourselves to be thy children, and to glorify thee as our Father, until we shall enjoy that eternal inheritance, through Christ our Lord. - Amen.

Jeremiah 35:8-16

Grant, Almighty God, that since thou hast made known to us by thy servants, not only once, and even often, the way of salvation, but hast sent also thine only-begotten Son to be to us a teacher of perfect wisdom, - O grant, that we may so submit to thee and so consecrate to thee our whole life, that he who died for our salvation and rose again, may peaceably rule us by the doctrine of his gospel; and that we may strive to glorify thee in this world, so that we may at last be made partakers of that celestial glory which the same thy Son our Lord has obtained for us. - Amen.

Jeremiah 35:17 – 36:6

Grant, Almighty God, that as we cease not continually to provoke thine anger against us, we may at length return to thee, and that every one may so examine his life, that being prostrate under a sense of thy wrath, we may betake ourselves to the only true remedy, even to implore thee, and to seek forgiveness; and do thou also so graciously meet us, that we may in sure faith call on thee, and, in the meantime, find really, by experience, that our prayers are not in vain, until we shall at length have a perfect enjoyment of thy mercy, in thy celestial kingdom. - Amen.

Jeremiah 36:7-16

Grant, Almighty God, that as thou art pleased to invite us daily to thyself, we may respond to thy call in the spirit of meekness and obedience; and do thou also so seriously impress our minds, that we may not only confess our sins, but also so loathe ourselves on account of them, that we may without delay seek the true remedy, and, relying on thy mercy, may so repent, that thy name may hereafter be glorified in us, until we shall at length become partakers of that glory, which thy Son has obtained for us by his own blood. - Amen.

Jeremiah 36:17-26

Grant, Almighty God, that since thou dost daily invite us kindly to thyself, and dost also terrify us in order to correct our tardiness and sloth, - O grant, that we may not obstinately resist thee and thy word, but be so allured by thy condescension and subdued by thy threatenings, that in real fear we may flee to thy mercy, and never hope for any other remedy, except we obtain salvation through being reconciled to thee, and that we may so seek thee in true penitence and by true faith, that thou mayest come to our aid, and be propitious to us through thine only-begotten Son our Lord. - Amen.

Jeremiah 36:27-32

Grant, Omnipotent God, that since thou warnest us by so remarkable examples, that the ungodly by obstinately resisting thee, do nothing but aggravate their own ruin, - O grant, that we may receive with meek hearts the admonitions of thy Prophets, and submit to thee, and be so humbled by thy threatenings and tremble at thy word, that being touched with the feeling of true repentance, and reconciled to thee by faith, we may find thee to be the best and the kindest Father to obedient children, until we shall at length enjoy that eternal inheritance which has been obtained for us by the blood of thine only-begotten Son. - Amen.

Jeremiah 37:1-10

Grant, omnipotent God, that as thou hast been pleased kindly to invite us to thyself, and settest before us the reconciliation which is through thine only-begotten Son, - O grant, that we may not proceed in our wickedness so as to provoke thee more and more against us, and to kindle the fire of thy vengeance on our own heads, but that we may so suhmit ourselves to thee, as to flee in sincere repentance and true faith to thy mercy, that we may find thee to be propitious to us, and that thou mayest thus afford us reason to give glory to thy name, having shewn mercy to us, through the same, thine only-begotten Son. - Amen.

Jeremiah 37:11-20

Grant, Almighty God, that as we must in various ways carry on a warfare on earth, we may be animated by the power of thy Spirit, so as to go on through fire and water, and be ever so subject to thee, that relying on thine aid, we may never hesitate to face all perils of death, all troubles, all reproaches, and all the terrors of men, until having at length gained the final victory, we shall come to that blessed rest, which thine only-begotten Son hath procured for us by his own blood. - Amen.

Jeremiah 37:21 – 38:5

Grant, Almighty God, that since thou invitest us daily to thyself with so much kindness, and givest us also time to repent, and then offerest to us the hope of mercy and salvation, if we return to thee, - O grant, that we may not pass by such benevolent warnings with deaf ears, but in due time attend to thee, and with true and sincere acknowledgment of all our sins so surrender up ourselves to thee, that we may find thee to be merciful; and that when we return to thee we may so continue in obedience to thee, that we may be capable of receiving thy constant kindness, until the full fruition of it shall be given us in thy celestial kingdom, through Christ our Lord. - Amen.

Jeremiah 38:6-14

Grant, omnipotent God, that since the life of thy servants ought to be deemed precious by us, each of us, according to his ability may strive to do his part in this respect, and, in the meantime, so cultivate mutual love as to assist one another in time of necessity, and that we may also be so solicitous respecting thy servants, as to consecrate all our efforts, all our labors, and all our services to thee, and strive thus to please thee, so that all our doings may be directed to this end, until, having at length finished the course of our present warfare, we shall come to that rest in thy celestial kingdom, which has been procured for us by the blood of thine only-begotten Son. - Amen.

Jeremiah 38:15-22

Grant, Almighty God, that since thou daily invitest us to repentance by constant exhortations, we may seriously reflect on thy goodness, and in due time return to thee and submit to thy will, and never refuse to undergo the punishment thou layest on us; and that we may not in the meantime so provoke thy extreme vengeance, as to find thee a rigorous judge, but ever experience, even under punishment, thy paternal mercy, until we shall at length come to the fullness of that joy which is laid up in heaven for us in Christ Jesus our Lord. - Amen.

Jeremiah 38:23 – 39:2

Grant, Almighty God, that as we are surrounded by so many dangers, and bring on ourselves daily, through our sins, so many miseries, - O grant, that we may at least yield to thy threatenings, and learn in due time to seek thy favor and to anticipate thy judgment, and so to humble ourselves under thy mighty hand, that we may find thee propitious to us miserable sinners, who flee to thy mercy, until, having at length been freed from all our sins, we shall appear before thy tribunal, and there receive the reward of our faith, even that blessed immortality, which thine only-begotten Son, our Lord, has procured for us by his own blood. - Amen.

Jeremiah 39:3-12

Grant, omnipotent God, that since thou hast once given us so awful a proof of thy wrath in the destruction of that city, which thou didst choose, and in which thou hadst had thy holy habitation, - O grant, that we may learn so to submit to thee in true humility and obedience, that we may not provoke thy extreme displeasure, but on the contrary anticipate it by real repentance, and that being terrified by thy threatenlugs, we may so submit ourselves to thee as to obtain thy mercy, and thus to regard thee as a Father, ever propitious to all those who flee to thee through Christ Jesus our Lord. - Amen.

Jeremiah 39:13 – 40:4

Grant, Almighty God, that as thou hast promised that we shall be to thee as the apple of the eye, - O grant, that we may ever flee under the shadow of thy mercy, and that this alone may be our tranquillity in times of confusion and misery: and may we, at the same time, recumb in confidence on thy help, that we may, in sincerity, perform what thou commandest us, and that which is our duty to do, so that we may, by experience, find, that all they who obey thy voice are really sustained by thine hand, and that those are never disappointed who look for the certain reward of their obedience from thee; and may we carry on the warfare so perseveringly in this life, that we may know that there is a reward laid up for us in heaven, when Christ thine only-begotten Son shall appear. - Amen.

Jeremiah 40:5-12

Grant, Almighty God, that as we are not sufficiently attentive in considering thy judgments, we may learn to become wise by the examples of others, and so to reflect on what thou teachest us by thy servants the Prophets, that we may apply it to our own use, and thus render ourselves teachable and obedient to thee, and that especially when thou chastisest us with thy scourges, we may not resist thy power, but so submit to thee, that we may at length be raised up and comforted by thy mercy and be restored to a complete salvation, through Christ Jesus our Lord. - Amen.

Jeremiah 40:13 – 41:5

Grant, omnipotent God, that since our life is exposed to innumerable dangers, and thou settest before our eyes what happened to the best and choicest of thy servants, - O grant, that we may flee to thee, and resign ourselves wholly to thy will, that we may know that thou art the guardian of our life, so that not a hair of our head can fall without thy hidden permission, and that we may also learn to ask of thee the spirit of wisdom and discretion, so that thou thyself mayest guide our steps, as it is not in us to defend our life from those many intrigues by which we are on every side surrounded, the whole world being opposed to us, so that we may proceed in the course of our pilgrimage under thy care and protection, until we shall be removed into that blessed rest, which is laid up for us in heaven by Christ our Lord. - Amen.

Jeremiah 41:6-15

Grant, omnipotent God, that as this world is filled with the filth of the wicked, and as we are on every side surrounded with enemies, - O grant, that we may learn to flee under thy protection, and so hide ourselves under the shadow of thy wings, that we may look nowhere else for safety but from thy defense; and that we may also know that as to everything that happens to us, our life and our death are so ordered by thy wonderful providence, that all events help forward our salvation, so that we may go onward, not only through many calamities, but, if need be, through the midst of slaughters, until we shall come to that blessed rest, which thine only-begotten Son has obtained for us by his own blood. - Amen.

Jeremiah 41:16 – 42:6

Grant, Almighty God, that as we are here tossed to and fro, being uncertain and doubtful, except we are ruled by thy word, and are blind in thick darkness, - O grant, that while thou shinest on us by thy Law and by thy Gospel, we may be illuminated as to our minds by thy Holy Spirit, so that we may wholly surrender ourselves to thee, and never deviate from the right way which thou hast made known to us, but so pursue our course through life, that at length we may come to that blessed life, which has been prepared for us in heaven by Jesus Christ our Lord. - Amen.

Jeremiah 42:7-17

Grant, Almighty God, that as thou hast not once only shown to us the way and the end to which we ought to proceed, but art pleased daily to stretch forth thy hand to us, and dost by thy constant exhortations invite and stimulate us to go onward, - O grant, that we may attend to thy voice, and so renounce all the corrupt desires and lusts of our flesh, that nothing may hinder us wholly to submit to thee, and so to follow whithersoever thou mayest call us, that we may at length come to that blessed rest, which thou hast prepared for us in heaven through Christ our Lord - Amen.

Jeremiah 42:18 – 43:3

Grant, Almighty God, that since we see what thou didst formerly threaten to all the despisers of thy word, we may learn to suffer ourselves to be ruled by thee, and so surrender all our powers and faculties to thy will, that we may receive immediately without any dispute whatever thou commandest, and so prove our sincerity, that our deeds may correspond with our words, and that our life may shew that we do not falsely profess thy holy name, but declare what we have in our minds and what thou thyself knowest, until the last day shall at length appear, when the books shall be opened, and all the thoughts of men shall be revealed, so that we may then appear upright in thy sight, through Christ our Lord. - Amen.

Jeremiah 43:4-12

Grant, Almighty God, that as thou hast not only once shewn to us the way in which we are to walk, but also daily exhortest us to continue in it, and ever to go forward towards the right mark, - O grant, that we may never turn aside, but suffer ourselves to be ruled by thy voice; and though temptations may drive us here and there, may we ever follow thy command, and so persevere in obedience to thee, that we may at length, by experience, find that it is our happiness to commit ourselves to thee, and to follow thee as our leader, until thou bringest us into that celestial kingdom, which has been prepared for us by thine only-begotten Son.-Amen.

Jeremiah 43:13 – 44:7

Grant, Almighty God, that since thou ceasest not continually to shew to us thy paternal love and care, - O grant, that we may not be so insensible as to turn a deaf ear to thy teaching and admonitions; but as thou watchest for our safety, may the constancy of our faith and obedience so respond to thee, that we may reverently receive thy word, suffer ourselves to be ruled by it, and follow the way which thou hast set before us, until we shall attain complete salvation, and enjoy that blessed inheritance which has been prepared for us in heaven by Christ our Lord. - Amen.

Jeremiah 44:8-16

Grant, Almighty God, that since thou wouldest prove our faith by many trials, we may constantly persevere in the pure worship of thy name, and in calling on thee in sincerity and truth, and that as we are surrounded and beset on every side by many pollutions, we may preserve ourselves pure and devoted to thee, both in body and soul, and thus proceed through the whole course of our life, so that at length we may appear unpolluted before thee, through Christ our Lord. - Amen.

Jeremiah 44:17-23

Grant, Almighty God, that as thou hast not only in thy Law prescribed to us what is right, and shewed to us the way of a godly life, but hast also more clearly revealed thy will to us by the light of thy Gospel, where Christ thy Son shines forth as the Sun of righteousness, - O grant, that we may submit ourselves wholly to thee, and from the heart render thee obedience, and to this apply all our efforts and direct all our doings, so that having finished the course of this life, we may at length come into that blessed rest which has been prepared for us in heaven by Christ our Lord. - Amen.

Jeremiah 44:24-30

Grant, Almighty God, that since by our adoption, thou hast favored us with this honor, that we may call on thy name, - O grant, that we may with a pure mouth call on thee, that thou mayest be glorified among us, through the whole course of our life; and that whilst we labor to render to thee that sincere obedience which thou requirest, thy truth may be more and more propagated among us, and that the memory of thy name may flourish more and more, until we shall at length come into that glory, which we know is laid up for us in heaven, by Christ our Lord. - Amen.

Jeremiah 45:1-5, 46:1-2

Grant, Almighty God, that since thou hast been pleased to call us to the spiritual warfare, we may never be wearied; and that, as our weakness is so great that we are unequal to our conflicts, grant, that being supported by the power of thy Spirit, we may persevere in the course of thy holy calling, and never be broken down by anything that may happen to us, but learn so to break through all dangers as to commit our life into thy hands, and be in the meantime prepared to live or to die, until thou gatherest us into that blessed rest which is laid up for us in heaven, through Christ our Lord. - Amen.

Jeremiah 46:3-12

Grant, Almighty God, that since we see that the most opulent kingdoms have not escaped thy hand, we may learn to recumb only on thine aid, and to submit ourselves to thee, with due hu-milky, so that we may be protected by thy hand, and that this only true confidence may sustain us in all perils, that thou hast undertaken the care of our salvation; and that we may, in the meantime, fight under thy banner with sincerity and uprightness of life, until we shall at length enjoy the fruit of our victory, in the celestial kingdom, through Christ our Lord. - Amen.

Jeremiah 46:13-21

Grant, Almighty God, that when thou indulgest us, we may not abuse thy patience, nor become wanton in prosperity, but learn so to subdue ourselves of our own accord, that we may obey thee through the whole course of our life, and mortify our flesh, lest we be elated by pride and false confidence, but so live in thy fear as to reverence thee when we regard thee as the righteous Judge of the world, and recumb at the same time on thee, when we acknowledge thee as our

Father, as thou hast been pleased to adopt us in thine only-begotten Son our Lord. - Amen.

Jeremiah 46:22-28

Grant, Almighty God, that as thou hast testified that thou wilt be a Father to us, and hast given us a pledge of thy adoption, thine only-begotten Son, - O grant, that we, trusting in thy promise, may never doubt, even when thou severely chastisest us, but that thou wilt at length be merciful to us, and that we may thus never cease to flee to thy mercy, and thus submit to thee, and suffer ourselves to be corrected; and may, in the meantime, this hope sustain us, and alleviate all our sorrows, that in all our miseries we shall yet ever glorify thy name, through the same, thy Son our Lord. - Amen.

Jeremiah 47:1-7

Grant, Almighty God, that as thou wouldst have to exist a monument of thine invaluable mercy towards thy chosen people, when thou didst so grievously punish the unbelieving, - O grant, that we may at this day resort to thee whenever our enemies distress us, and never doubt but that thou wilt take care of our safety, and so recumb on thy mercy, that we may patiently wait for the time of our deliverance; and that, in the meantime, we may see from on high, as in mirror, the punishment prepared for the unbelieving, so that we may not follow their example nor implicate ourselves in their vices, but separate ourselves from them, that, being devoted to thee, we may fight under the banner of thine only-begotten Son, until he shall gather us into his celestial kingdom. - Amen.

Jeremiah 48:1-11

Grant, Almighty God, that since we are so disposed to indulge sloth, and so devoted to earthly things, that we easily forget our holy calling except thou dost continually stimulate us, - O grant that the afflictions by which thou triest us, may effectually rouse us, so that leaving the world we may strive to come to thee, and devote ourselves wholly to thy service; and that we may so carry on the warfare under the various afflictions of the present life, that our minds and all our thoughts may always be fixed on the hope of that eternal and blessed rest which thine only-begotten Son our Lord has promised as having been prepared for us in heaven. - Amen.

Jeremiah 48:12-27

Grant Almighty God, that we may learn, not only to consider thy judgments when they appear before our eyes, but also to fear them whenever they are announced, so that we may implore thy mercy, and also repent of our sins and patiently bear thy paternal chastisements, and never murmur when thou sparest for a time the ungodly, but wait with calm and resigned minds until the time comes when thou wilt execute vengeance on them, and when in the meantime thou wilt gather us at the end of our warfare into the blessed rest above, and give us to enjoy that inheritance which thou hast prepared for us in Heaven, and which has been obtained for us by the blood of thine only-begotten Son our Lord. - Amen.

Jeremiah 48:28-35

Grant, Almighty God, that since thou hast once deigned to receive us under thy protection, we may have thee as our defense against our enemies, and that the more cruel and ferocious they become, and that the more heavily thou chastisest them, we may thus find that thou carest for our salvation, and flee also to thee with greater confidence, and that when we have experienced thy mercy, we may more readily give thee continual thanks, through Christ Jesus our Lord. - Amen.

Jeremiah 48:36-47

Grant, Almighty God, that as thou wert formerly pleased to extend thy mercy to aliens, who were wholly estranged from thee, that the children of Abraham, whom thou didst adopt, might hence have a hope of deliverance, - O grant, that we may also, at this day, cast our eyes on the many proofs of thy goodness, manifested towards the ungodly and the unworthy, so as to make an application for our own benefit, and never to doubt but that however miserable we may be, thou wilt yet be ever propitious to us, since thou hast deigned to choose us for thy peculiar people, and hast promised to be ever our God and Father in Christ Jesus our Lord. - Amen.

Jeremiah 49:1-6

Grant, Almighty God, that as thou didst formerly give so many proofs how great and singular was thy love towards the children of Abraham, whom it had pleased thee to choose as thy people, - O grant that we at this day may also enjoy the same favor, since we have been admitted into a participation of the same union, and that we may be so chastised as never to lose the hope of thy mercy, but that we may so taste it as to meditate on that celestial kingdom, which has been obtained for us by the blood of thine only-begotten Son. - Amen.

Jeremiah 49:7-12

Grant, Almighty God, that as thou hast not only in thine eternal counsel adopted us as thy children, but hast also inscribed on our hearts a sure sign and pledge of thy paternal favor towards us, - O grant that we may accustom ourselves to bear thy scourges, and patiently to receive them without murmuring or complaining, but that we may ever look forward to the blessed rest and inheritance above, and at the same time dread the punishment that awaits the wicked, and that we may thus courageously persevere in our warfare, until thou at length gatherest us into that celestial kingdom which thine only-begotten Son has procured for us by his own blood. - Amen.

Jeremiah 49:13-18

Grant, Almighty God, that as thou hast been pleased to stretch forth thine hand to us, we may be raised by faith above the world, and learn to submit to thee in true humility, and to know how miserable must be our condition and life, except we wholly recumb on thee alone, so that we may be made partakers of that glory which thou hast purchased for us in Heaven, and which thine only-begotten Son, our Lord, has obtained for us. - Amen.

Jeremiah 49:19-23

Grant, Almighty God, that as thou settest before our eyes memorable judgments which ought to benefit us at this day, so that we may be kept under thy yoke and under the fear of thy law, - O grant, that we may not grow hard at such threatenings, but anticipate thy wrath, and so submit to thee, that whatever thou denouncest on the ungodly may turn to our comfort, and for a cause of joy, when we know that the salvation of thy church is thus promoted, of which thou hast been pleased to regard and acknowledge us as members in thy Son our Lord. - Amen.

Jeremiah 49:24-32

Grant, Almighty God, that though the things related to us today from thy Prophets, concerning ancient nations, may seem as grown out of use, O grant that we may however be seriously impressed whenever we read of thy judgments as executed on any part of the world, so that we may learn at this day wholly to submit to thee and flee to thy mercy, and that whatever may happen to us, we may never doubt but that thou wilt be propitious to us, if we seek thee with a sincere heart, and with unfeigned faith in Christ Jesus, our Lord. - Amen.

Jeremiah 49:33-39

Grant, Almighty God, that as thou didst favor despairing men with some consolation when justly and extremely indignant with them, - O grant that whenever we at this day provoke thy wrath, we may at the same time taste of thy paternal mercy, and learn to flee to thee, and to put our hope in thine only-begotten Son, so that we may never despond, but ever look forward to that gathering, whose beginning is now seen, and whose final and complete accomplishment awaits us in heaven, through the same Christ our Lord. - Amen.

Jeremiah 50:1-6

Grant, Almighty God, that we may not be inebriated with the sweetness of earthly blessings which thou bestowest continually on us, but learn to ascend to the hope of celestial life and eternal felicity, and in the meantime have such a taste of thy blessings, that we may know that thou art an inexhaustible fountain of all felicity, so that we may cleave to thee with a sincere heart and in perfect integrity, until we shall at length be brought to the full fruition of that kingdom, which thine only-begotten Son has procured for us by his own blood. - Amen.

Jeremiah 50:7-12

Grant, Almighty God, that though we cease not daily to provoke thy wrath by our many sins, we may yet, with confidence, flee to thy mercy, and that though thou seemest for a time to cast us away, we may not yet cast away hope, founded on thy eternal word, but that, relying on that Mediator in whom we always find the price of expiation, we may not hesitate to call on thee as our Father; and may we, in the meantime, find thee by experience to be such towards us, so that we may cheerfully look forward to that celestial inheritance, which has been obtained for us by the blood of thy only-begotten Son. - Amen.

Jeremiah 50:13-20

Grant, Almighty God, that since thou hast been so merciful towards thine ancient people, and however grievously thou mightest have been offended, yet thou didst preserve some remnant to whom thou gavest tokens of thy mercy, - O grant that it may please thee so to allure us also at this day; and however we may deserve a thousand times to be condemned by thee, yet deign to receive us in thine only-begotten Son, and through him show thyself reconciled to us to the end of our life; and be thou our Father in death itself, so that we may live and die to thee, and acknowledge this to be the only true way of salvation, until we shall at length enjoy that celestial inheritance which has been obtained for us by the blood of the same, thine only-begotten Son. - Amen.

Jeremiah 50:21-25

Grant, Almighty God, that since thou hast been pleased to set before us thy judgments on the unbelieving, we may not only fear thee, but also learn to cast on thee the hope of our salvation, so that we may make progress in the truth, that we may neither be insensible as to thy threatenings, nor tremble in our extreme evils, but so learn to raise up to thee our eyes, that we may, during the whole course of our life, call on thee through Christ Jesus our Lord. - Amen.

Jeremiah 50:26-34

Grant, Almighty God, that, as thou hast deigned once to take us under thy protection, we may always raise up our eyes to thine infinite power, and that when we see all things not only confounded, but also trodden under foot by the world, we may not yet doubt but that thy power is sufficient to deliver us, so that we may perpetually call on thy name, and with firm constancy so fight against all temptations, that we may at length enjoy in thy celestial kingdom the fruit of our victory, through Jesus Christ our Lord. - Amen.

Jeremiah 50:35-42

Grant, Almighty God, that since thou teachest us by the example of the ungodly to fear thy name, we may learn to submit our necks to thy word, and willingly, and as it becomes us, submissively to receive thy yoke, that while we strive to glorify thy name, being safe under thy protection, we may disregard all the attacks of our enemies, and all the assaults and onsets of Satan, who is the captain of all our enemies, until we shall at length enjoy our victory in the celestial kingdom, through Christ our Lord. - Amen.

Jeremiah 50:43 – 51:3

Grant Almighty God, that since thou wert formerly so solicitous respecting the salvation of thy people as to undertake war, for their sake, against a most powerful nation, - O grant, that we also, at this day, may know, that we shall be safe and secure under the protection of thy hand, and that we may so experience thy power, that there may be to us a just reason for glorying in thee, and that our enemies may be confounded, in order that thy glory may shine forth more and more, and that the kingdom of thine only-begotten Son may also be thus promoted. - Amen.

Jeremiah 51:4-10

Grant, Almighty God, that since thou didst formerly put forth thy wonderful power, to help thy miserably afflicted people, - O grant, that at this day the same power may be put forth in our behalf, and that the same evidence of thy grace and paternal favor may be shown to us, by raising up thy terrible hand to destroy all the ungodly who cruelly oppress thine innocent people, that being delivered by thine hand, we may learn ever to give thanks to thee, in the name of thine only-begotten Son. - Amen.

Jeremiah 51:11-16

Grant, Almighty God, that since thou hast deigned once to receive us under thy protection, we may learn to recumb on the power of thy hand, and that as so many terrors on every side meet us through the assaults and cruelty of our enemies, we may yet continue firm, and persevere in calling on thy name, until thou appearest as our Redeemer, not only once, but whenever we may need thy help, until thou gatherest us at length into that blessed rest, which has been prepared for us in heaven, through Christ our Lord. - Amen.

Jeremiah 51:17-24

Grant, Almighty God, that since thou hast favored us with the light of thy Gospel, in which we see thy glory, and into which we may be also transformed, except prevented by our unbelief, - O grant, that with fixed eyes we may ever study that knowledge which once for all has been made known to us, until at length, having followed the way there set before us, we shall come to the fullness of that celestial glory which has been obtained for us by the blood of thine only-begotten Son. - Amen.

Jeremiah 51:25-32

Grant, Almighty God, that as thou didst formerly testify thy favor towards thy Church by not sparing the greatest of monarchies, - O grant that we may know thee at this day to be the same towards all thy faithful people who call upon thee; and as the power and cruelty of our enemies are so great, raise thou up thine hand against them, and show that thou art the perpetual defender of thy Church, so that we may have reason to magnify thy goodness in Christ Jesus our Lord. - Amen.

Jeremiah 51:33-41

Grant, Almighty God, that since thou art pleased at this day to receive us for thy people, we may enjoy the same favor to the end, and be sheltered under thy wings; and though we deserve to be wholly cast away, yet, if thou chastise us for a time, deal with us with moderate severity, and chastise us in judgment, and not with extreme rigor; and then, after darkness, let thy serene face appear, until we shall at length enjoy that full light to which thou invitest us daily through Christ Jesus our Lord. - Amen.

Jeremiah 51:42-48

Grant, Almighty God, that since thou not only testifiest to us that thou wilt be the Redeemer of thy Church, into which thou hast been pleased to introduce us, but hast also really manifested thyself to us in thine only-begotten Son, - O grant that we may patiently bear all the contests and afflictions by which thou now provest our faith, and that we may perseveringly fight under the cross, until, having gone through all our trials, we shall at length enjoy eternal glory, when we shall find thee to be our complete Redeemer, through the same Christ Jesus our Lord. - Amen.

Jeremiah 51:49-56

Grant, Almighty God, that when thou hidest at this day thy face from us, the miserable despair we apprehend may not overwhelm our faith, nor obscure our view of thy goodness and grace, but that in the thickest darkness thy power may ever appear to us, which can raise us above the world, so that we may courageously fight to the end, and never doubt but that thou wilt at length be the defender of thy Church, which now seems to be oppressed, until we shall enjoy our perfect happiness in heaven, through Christ our Lord. - Amen.

Jeremiah 51:57-64

Grant, Almighty God, that Since thou hast deigned to choose us for thy people, we may not doubt but that our enemies will be before thee like Babylon, so that when thou hast chastised us, thou wilt at length, by a fatal and perpetual destruction, so lay them prostrate, that they shall rise up no more; and when thou hast killed the body, manifest thyself as our deliverer, until we shall at length be gathered into that celestial kingdom which has been prepared for us by thine only-begotten Son. - Amen.

The last chapter, as it is historical, and all its parts have been elsewhere handled, Calvin did not expound in his Lectures, that he might not burden the hearers with superfluous repetitions, so there are no prayers for this chapter.

LAMENTATIONS

Lamentations 1:1-5

Grant, Almighty God, that as the deformity of thy Church at this day is sufficient to dishearten us all, we may learn to look to thine hand, and know that the reward of our sins is rendered to us, and that we may not doubt but that thou wilt be our physician to heal our wound, provided we flee to thy mercy; and do thou so retain us in the assurance of thy goodness and paternal care, that we may not hesitate, even in extreme evils, to call on thee in the name of thine only-begotten Son, until we shall find by experience that never in vain are the prayers of those, who, relying on thy promises, patiently look for a remedy from thee alone, even in extreme evils, and also in death itself. - Amen.

Lamentations 1:6-10

Grant, Almighty God, that as at this day we see thy Church miserably afflicted, we may direct our eyes so as to see our own sins, and so humble ourselves before thy throne, that we may yet cease not to, entertain hope, and in the midst of death wait for life; and may this confidence open our mouth, that we may courageously persevere in calling on thy name, through Christ our Lord. - Amen.

Lamentations 1:11-18

Grant, Almighty God, that as thou hast hitherto dealt so mercifully with us, we may anticipate thy dreadful judgment; and that if thou shouldest more severely chastise us, we may not yet fail, but that being humbled under thy mighty hand, we may flee to thy mercy and cherish this hope in our hearts, that thou wilt be a Father to us, and not hesitate to call continually on thee, until, being freed from all evils, we shall at length be gathered into thy celestial kingdom, which thine only Son has procured for us by his own blood. - Amen.

Lamentations 1:19 – 2:2

Grant, Almighty God, that as thou settest before us at this day those ancient examples by which we perceive with what heavy punishments thou didst chastise those whom thou hadst adopted, - O grant, that we may learn to regard thee, and carefully to examine our whole life, and duly consider how indulgently thou hast preserved us to this day, so that we may ever patiently bear thy chastisements, and with a humble and sincere heart flee to thy mercy, until thou be pleased to raise up thy Church from that miserable state in which it now lies, and so to restore it, that thy name may, through thine only-begotten Son, be glorified throughout the whole world. - Amen.

Lamentations 2:3-9

Grant, Almighty God, that since so many tokens of thy wrath meet us at this day, we may without delay return to thee, and so submit to thee in true repentance, as to strive at the same time to be reconciled to thee; and as a Mediator has been given to us to lead us to thee, - O grant that we may by a true faith seek him, and follow wherever he may call us, that having been purified from all pollution's, we may be glorified by thee our Father, and may so call on thee, that we may find thy grace present in all our evils. Amen.

Lamentations 2:10-14

Grant, Almighty God, that though thou chastisest us as we deserve, we may yet never have the light of truth extinguished among us, but may ever see, even in darkness, at least some sparks, which may enable us to behold thy paternal goodness and mercy, so that we may especially be humbled under thy mighty hand, and that being really prostrate through a deep feeling of repentance, we may raise our hopes to heaven, and never doubt but that thou wilt at length be reconciled to us when we seek thee in thine only-begotten Son. - Amen.

Lamentations 2:15-20

Grant, Almighty God, that as thy Church at this day is oppressed with many evils, we may learn to raise up not only our eyes and our hands to thee, but also our hearts, and that we may so fix our attention on thee as to look for salvation from thee alone; and that though despair may overwhelm us on earth, yet the hope of thy goodness may ever shine on us from heaven, and that, relying on the Mediator whom thou hast given us, we may not hesitate to cry continually to thee, until we really find by experience that our prayers have not been ill vain, when thou, pitying thy Church, hast extended thy hand, and given us cause to rejoice, and hast turned our mourning into joy, through Christ our Lord. - Amen.

Lamentations 2:21 – 3:9

Grant, Almighty God, that as thou didst in former times so severely chastise thy people, we may in the present day patiently submit to all thy scourges, and in a humble and meek spirit suffer ourselves to be chastised as we deserve; and that we may not, in the meantime, cease to call on thee, and that however slowly thou mayest seem to hear our prayers, we may yet persevere continually to the end, until at length we shall really find that salvation is not in vain promised to all those who in sincerity of heart call on thee, through Christ our Lord. - Amen.

Lamentations 3:10-23

Grant, Almighty God, that as there are none of us who have not continually to contend with many temptations, and as such is our infirmity, that we are ready to succumb under them, except thou helpest us, - O grant, that we may be sustained by thine invincible power, and that also, when thou wouldest humble us, we may loathe ourselves on account of our sins, and thus perseveringly contend, until, having gained the victory, we shall give thee the glory for thy perpetual aid in Christ Jesus our Lord. - Amen.

Lamentations 3:24-31

Grant, Almighty God, that as it is expedient for us to be daily chastised by thy hand, we may willingly submit to thee, and not doubt but that thou wilt be faithful, and not prove us with too much rigor, but that thou wilt consider our weakness, so that we may thus calmly bear all thy chastisements, until we shall at length enjoy that perfect blessedness, which is now hid to us under hope, and as it were sealed, until Christ thy Son shall reveal it at his coming. - Amen.

Lamentations 3:32-39

Grant, Almighty God, that as we are at this day tossed here and there by so many troubles, and almost all things in the world are in confusion, so that wherever we turn our eyes, nothing but thick darkness meets us, - O grant that we may learn to surmount all obstacles, and to raise our eyes by faith above the world, so that we may acknowledge that governed by thy wonderful counsel is everything that seems to us to happen by chance, in order that we may seek thee, and know that help will be ready for us through thy mercy whenever we humbly seek the pardon of our sins, through Christ Jesus our Lord. - Amen.

Lamentations 3:40-51

Grant, Almighty God, that as thou hast hitherto spared us, we may not grow torpid in our vices, and that since thou hast already begun to deal more severely with thy Church, we may be awakened by thy chastisements, and so humble ourselves under thy mighty hand, as yet not to doubt but that thou wilt be propitions to us, and that we may so loathe ourselves on account of our sins, as still to be fully persuaded that, provided we wait for thee, thou wilt at length be merciful to us, so as to afford us new reasons for joy and gratitude, through Christ Jesus our Lord. - Amen.

Lamentations 3:52-66

Grant, Almighty God, that as at this day ungodly men and wholly reprobate so arrogantly rise up against thy Church, we may learn to flee to thee, and to hide ourselves under the shadow of thy wings, and fully to hope for thy salvation; and that however disturbed the state of things may be, we may yet never doubt but that thou wilt be propitious to us, since we have so often found thee to be our deliverer; and that we may thus persevere in confidence of thy grace and mercy, and be also roused by this incentive to pray to thee, until having gone through all our miseries, we shall at length enjoy that blessed rest which thou hast promised to us through Christ Jesus our Lord. - Amen.

Lamentations 4:1-9

Grant. Almighty God, that as thou shewest by thy Prophet that, after having long borne with thine ancient people, thy wrath at length did so far burn as to render final judgment above all others remarkable, - O grant that we may not at this day, by our obstinacy or by our sloth, provoke thy wrath, but be attentive to thy threatenings, yea, and obey thy paternal invitations, and so willingly devote ourselves to thy service, that as thou hast hitherto favored us with thy blessings, so thou mayest perpetuate them, until we shall at length enjoy the fullness of all good things in thy celestial kingdom, through Christ our Lord. - Amen.

Lamentations 4:10-17

Grant, Almighty God, that as we are beset on every side with so many allurements, and as Satan ceases not to draw us here and there by vain flatteries, - O grant that we may recumb on thee alone, even on thy power, and, in short, on thy word, nor doubt but thou wilt be our deliverer, whatever may happen, and that we may always so seek thee in our straits, and so acquiesce in the faithfulness of thy promises, that we may calmly sustain all the assaults of afflictions, until thou at length gatherest us into that blessed rest which is prepared for us in heaven by Christ our Lord. - Amen.

Lamentations 4:18-22

Grant, Almighty God, that as thou seest that at this day the mouths not only of our enemies, but of thine also, are open to speak evil, - O grant, that no occasion may be given them, especially as their slanders are cast on thy holy name; but restrain thou their insolence, and so spare us, that though we deserve to be chastised, thou mayest yet have regard for thine own glory, and thus gather us under Christ our head, and restore thy scattered Church, until we shall at length be all gathered into that celestial kingdom, which thine only-begotten Son our Lord has procured for us by his own blood. - Amen.

Lamentations 5:1-13

Grant, Almighty God, that since thou hast once stretched forth thy hand to consecrate us a people to thyself, - O grant, that thy favor may perpetually shine on us, and that we may, on the other hand, strive always to glorify thy name, so that having once embraced us thou mayest continue thy goodness, until we shall at length enjoy the fullness of all blessings in thy celestial kingdom, which has been obtained for us by the blood of thine only-begotten Son. - Amen.

Lamentations 5:14-22

Grant, Almighty God, that as thou didst formerly execute judgments so severe on thy people, - O grant, that these chastisements may at this day teach us to fear thy name, and also keep us in watchfulness and humility, and that we may so strive to pursue the course of our calling, that we may find that thou art always our leader, that thy hand is stretched forth to us, that thy aid is ever ready for us, until, being at length gathered into thy celestial kingdom, we shall enjoy that eternal life, which thine only-begotten Son has obtained for us by his own blood. - Amen.

EZEKIEL

Ezekiel 1:1-3

Grant, Almighty God, since thou didst bless thy people with the continued grace of thy Spirit when it was cast out of its inheritance, and didst raise up a Prophet even from the lowest depths, who should recall it to life when it was all but despaired of -- O grant, that although the Church in these days is miserably afflicted by thy hand, we may not be destitute of thy consolation, but show us, through thy pity, that life may be looked for even in the midst of death; so that we may bear all thy chastisements patiently, until thou shalt show thyself our reconciled Father, and thus at length we may be gathered into that happy kingdom, where we shall enjoy our full felicity, in Jesus Christ our Lord. -- Amen

Ezekiel 1:4-9

Almighty God, since by our dullness we are so fixed down to earth that, when thou stretchest forth thine hand to us, we cannot reach forth to thee, grant, that being roused up by thy Spirit, we may learn to raise our affections to thee, and to strive against our sluggishness, until by a nearer approach thou mayest become so familiarly known to us, that at length we may arrive at the fruition of full and perfect glory laid up for us in heaven, through Jesus Christ our Lord. Amen

Ezekiel 1:10-16

Grant, O Almighty God, since thou wishest us to be subject to so many changes, that we cannot settle on earth with quiet minds -- grant, I pray thee, that, being subject to so varying a condition, we may seek our rest in heaven, and always aspire to behold thy glory, so that what our eyes cannot discern may shine upon us from thence; and may we so acknowledge thy hand and power in the government of the whole world, that we may repose upon thy paternal care till we arrive at the enjoyment of that happy rest Which has been acquired for us by the blood of thine only begotten Son. -- Amen

Ezekiel 1:17-24

Grant, Almighty God, that though we have wandered far from thee, we may be taught by thy word, and hold on in the right way of approach to thyself, and by faith contemplate what is otherwise hidden from us, and thus depend entirely on thee. May we so rely on thy providence, as not to doubt our perfect safety while our life and salvation are in thy care, so that while tossed about by various storms we may remain quiet, until at length we enjoy that blessed and eternal rest which thou hast prepared for us in heaven by Jesus Christ our Lord. Amen

Ezekiel 1:25-28

Grant, O Almighty God, since of thine unbounded goodness, thou hast counted us worthy of such honor as to descend to earth in the person of thine only-begotten Son, and to appear familiarly to us daily in thy gospel, in which we contemplate thy living image: -- grant, I pray thee, that we may not abuse so great a benefit to vain curiosity, but may be truly transformed into thy glory, and so proceed more and more in the renewal of our mind and conduct, that we may at length be gathered to that eternal glory which has been obtained for us by thine only-begotten Son our Lord. Amen

Ezekiel 2:1-5

Grant, O Almighty God, since thou hast counted us worthy of enjoying the privilege of daily listening to thy word, that it may not find our hearts of stone and our minds of iron, but may we so submit ourselves to thee with all due docility, that we may truly perceive thee to be our Father, and may be confirmed in the confidence of our adoption, as long as thou perseverest to address us, until at length we enjoy not merely thy voice, but also the aspect of thy glory in thy heavenly kingdom, which thine only-begotten Son has acquired for us by his blood. -- Amen

Ezekiel 2:6-9

Grant, Almighty God, since thou hast this day deigned to invite us to thyself with the testimony of thy paternal favor, that we may not be as the beasts of the forest, but submit ourselves calmly to thee, and so follow where thou callest us, that we may in reality feel thee to be our Father; and thus may we live under the protection of thy hand as long as we are pilgrims in this world, so that at length being gathered unto thy heavenly kingdom, we may cleave entirely to thee and thine only-begotten Son, who is our felicity and glory. -- Amen

Ezekiel 3:1-11

Grant, Almighty God, since thou art desirous that the teaching of thy Prophet should be set before us, so many ages after his death, that we be not either obdurate or rebellious; but may we submit ourselves to thee in all becoming reverence and obedience, that the labor which ended in the condemnation of thine ancient people, through their contumacy, may this day be salutary to us, and may we so follow what thou teachest through him, that we may tend to the goal to which thou callest us, until after finishing our course with perseverance, we may be at length gathered together within thy celestial kingdom, through Christ our Lord. -- Amen

Ezekiel 3:12-17

Grant, Almighty God, since thou condescendest to interest thyself in our salvation, and stirrest up thy servants to be to us instead of eyes, that we may know thy watchfulness over us lest we perish, -- grant, I pray thee, that we may be so roused by the holy admonitions which flow from thee through their ministry and service, that if we have turned aside from the right way we may speedily return to it, and so go forward in our course, and be endued with such perseverance, that we may at length arrive at the fruition of that blessed rest, which has been obtained for us by the blood of thy Son. Amen

Ezekiel 3:18-20

O Almighty God, grant, that as thou dost appoint the ministers of thy doctrine, whom thou dost raise up, watchmen over us on this condition, that they be vigilant for our safety, -- grant that we also may be attentive to their instructions, and avoid a double destruction through our own fault, by error and obstinacy; but if we should happen to wander, may we be wise again immediately we are blamed, and so return into the right way, as never to desert it again, but persevere unto the end, that we may at length enjoy that eternal blessedness which is laid up for us in heaven, through Christ our Lord. Amen

Ezekiel 3:21 – 4:1-3

Grant, Almighty God, since thou so graciously invitest us to thee, and ceasest not, even if we are deaf, to continue towards us the same goodness -- that at length we may be disciplined to obedience and permit ourselves to be ruled by thy word: grant also that we may obey not only for a single day or a short period, but perseveringly, until at the final close of life's journey we may be gathered at length to thy celestial repose, through Jesus Christ our Lord. Amen

Ezekiel 4:4-11

Almighty God, since thou hast thus far sustained us by thy inestimable clemency, grant that we may not abuse thy goodness, and by our perverseness provoke thy vengeance against us, but may we prevent thy judgment, and so submit ourselves to thee that thou mayest take us into thy confidence and protect us against all our enemies: then supply us bountifully with whatever is needful for us, and since thou wishest us to restrain our natural desires, may we never be deficient in spiritual food, but be continually refreshed with it, until at length we enjoy that fullness which is promised us and laid up for us in heaven by Christ our Lord. -- Amen

Ezekiel 4:12-13 – 5:1-4

Grant, Almighty God, since thou hast proclaimed such a proof of thy fierce anger against thine ancient people, that we may this day learn wisdom from the suffering of others, and may so subject ourselves obediently to thee, that thou mayest receive us into favor, and show thyself so propitious to us, that by thy pardon we may be restored from death to life, until we enjoy that eternal blessedness which is provided for us by thine only-begotten Son our Lord. -- Amen

Ezekiel 5:5-11

Grant, Almighty God, since at this time thou hast so familiarly manifested thyself to us in the gospel of Christ our Lord, that we may learn to raise our eyes to the light which has been prepared for us; and grant that we may have them so fixed that we may be directed and urged towards the object of our existence, until the duties of our calling being finished, we may arrive at length unto thee, and enjoy also with thee that glory which thine only-begotten Son acquired for us by his blood. -- Amen

Ezekiel 5:12-17

Grant, Almighty God, since we are so dull and heavy, that we may awake in time at thy threats, and submit ourselves to thy power, that we may not experience by our destruction how formidable it is, but profit under thy rod when thou correctest us like a father, and may we so become wise, that through the whole course of our life we may proceed in the continual pursuit and meditation of true repentance; and having put off the vices and filth of the flesh, we may be reformed into true purity, until at length we arrive at the enjoyment of celestial glow, which is laid up for us in Christ Jesus our Lord. -- Amen

Ezekiel 6:1-9

Grant, Almighty God, since thou desirest a continual memorial of thy former remarkable judgments on thy people, that we may this day restrict ourselves to thy pure worship -- grant, I say, that we may be teachable by thee, and never attempt to adulterate thy worship by our devices; and since thou hast clearly manifested thy will to us, through thine only-begotten Son, that we may remain in obedience to him, and may so invoke Thee the Father, in his name, while we are pilgrims in the world, until at length we arrive at that blessed inheritance which is laid up for us in heaven by the same, our Lord. -- Amen

Ezekiel 6:10-13

Grant, Almighty God, since thou not only proposest to us this day the ancient examples of thine anger, by which we may be restrained within thy pure and perfect worship, but also hast so clearly manifested thyself to us, through thine only-begotten Son, that we cannot err unless we are insane, -- grant, I say, that we may be not only docile and moral, but attentive to that doctrine which is contained in thy gospel, so that we may be directed by this perfect light, until we arrive at length at the full and solid alliance with the Sun of righteousness, Christ, thy Son. -- Amen

Ezekiel 6:14 – 7:8

Grant, Almighty God, that we being admonished by such remarkable proofs of thy wrath, may learn to walk anxiously in thy sight, and so to bring ourselves into voluntary obedience to thyself, that the certain testimony to our gratuitous adoption may appear in our life; and grant that we may so prove ourselves to be sons, that we may truly invoke thee the Father, until we arrive at that blessed inheritance which has been obtained for us by the blood of thine only-begotten Son. -- Amen

Ezekiel 7:9-18

Grant, Almighty God, since thou hast recalled us to thyself, that we may not grow torpid in our sins, nor yet become hardened by thy chastisements, but prevent in time thy final judgments, and so humble ourselves under thy powerful hand, that we may seriously testify and really prove our repentance, and so study to obey thee, that we may advance in newness of life more and more, until at length we put off all the defilements of the flesh, and arrive at the enjoyment of that eternal rest which thine only-begotten Son has acquired for us by his own blood, -- Amen

Ezekiel 7:19-26

Grant, Almighty God, since thou hast hitherto deigned to guard us safely by thy power, and hast driven away so many violent assaults from us, and turned away so many perverse counsels of our enemies, and snatched us from numberless evils, -- grant that we may so value thy benefits towards us that we may be grateful in return, and so devote ourselves obediently to thee, that thy holy name may be glorified through our whole life in thy only-begotten Son our Lord. -- Amen

Ezekiel 7:27 – 8:6

Grant, Almighty God, since thou hast treated us so indulgently, and when provoked by our iniquities, hast yet shown thyself a propitious Father to us, that we may no longer abuse thy patience, but return directly to thy way and submit ourselves to thee -- and, being humbled by a true sense of penitence, grant that we may be so dissatisfied with our sins, that we may devote ourselves to thee with our whole heart and follow the direction of thy holy calling; until after finishing the pursuits of this rife, we may arrive at that happy repose which thine only-begotten Son has acquired for us by his blood. -- Amen

Ezekiel 8:7-14

Grant, Almighty God, since thou hast delivered to us a sure rule of worship, which cannot deceive us, and since thy Son became for us a perfect master of all wisdom and of solid piety, that we may obediently follow whatever he prescribes for us, and turn neither to the right hand nor the left; but being content with that simplicity which we have learnt from his Gospel, may go on in the course of our holy calling, until at length, that pursuit being finished, we may arrive at the perfect state of thy glory, and may so enjoy it that we may be transformed into it, as thou hast promised us by the same Jesus Christ our Lord. -- Amen

Ezekiel 8:15-16 – 9:4

Grant, Almighty God, since thou hast deigned to approach us so familiarly, that in return we may also desire to approach thee, and remain in firm and holy union; so that whilst we persevere in that lawful course which thou prescribest for us in thy word, thy blessings may increase towards us, until thou leadest us to fullness, when thou shalt gather us into thy celestial kingdom, by Christ our Lord. -- Amen

Ezekiel 9:5-9

Grant, Almighty God, since thou didst formerly chastise thy people so harshly, that we may profit by their example; and may we be so restrained by fear of thy name and obedience to thy law, that thou mayest not pour forth thy wrath against us: then if thou chastisest us, grant that it may all turn out to our good: and may we so feel ourselves to have been sealed by thee, and to be acknowledged in the number of thy sons, until at length thou shalt gather us into that blessed inheritance which has been obtained for us by the blood of thine only-begotten Son. -- Amen

Ezekiel 9:10-11 – 10:5

Grant, Almighty God, since thou now placest before our eyes proofs of thine anger, that we may not perversely provoke thy wrath, like thine ancient people; but rather, may we so profit by this teaching as to grow wise in time, and strive to be reconciled to thee, and to cast away all our depraved desires, until at length we shall be gathered unto that blessed rest which thine only-begotten Son has procured for us by his blood. -- Amen

Ezekiel 10:6-16

Grant, Almighty God, since we are the work of thy hands, that we may know that we exist and move in thee alone, so that we may submit ourselves to thee, and not only may we be ruled by thy hidden providence, but may it so appear that we are obedient and submissive to thee, as becometh sons, that we may desire to glorify thy name in the world, until we arrive at the fruition of that blessed inheritance which is laid up for us in heaven, through Christ our Lord. -- Amen

Ezekiel 10:17-22 – 11:3

Grant, Almighty God, that as we know from thine ancient people how great our hardness is, unless we are inclined by thy Holy Spirit, nay, totally renewed into obedience to thy doctrine: that as often as we hear thy threatening, we may be seriously frightened, and that we may desire to return to true and perfect obedience, not by momentary but by permanent repentance, till at length we are gathered into that happy rest, which has been obtained for us through the blood of thine only-begotten Son. Amen

Ezekiel 11:4-13

Grant, Almighty God, since we cease not to provoke thine anger every day, that at least being admonished by the prophecies which thine ancient people did not despise with impunity, we may be touched with a true sense of penitence, and may we so submit ourselves to thee, that we may willingly humble and renounce ourselves; and not only do thou mitigate the punishments which otherwise hang over us, but also show thyself a merciful and gracious Father towards us, until at length we enjoy the fullness of thy fatherly love in thy heavenly kingdom, through Christ our Lord. -- Amen

Ezekiel 11:14-20

Grant, O Almighty God, that we may learn to cast our eyes upon the state of thine ancient Church, since at the present day the sorrowful and manifest dispersion of thy Church seems to threaten its complete destruction: Grant also, that we may look upon those promises which are common to us also, that we may wait till thy Church emerges again from the darkness of death. Meanwhile, may we be content with thy help, however weak as to outward appearance, till at length it shall appear that our patience was not delusive, when we enjoy the reward of our faith and patience in thy heavenly kingdom, through Jesus Christ our Lord. -- Amen

Ezekiel 11:21

Grant, Almighty God, since we have utterly perished in our father Adam, and there remains in us no single part which is not corrupt, whilst we carry material for wrath, and cursing, and death, as well in the soul as in the body, that being regenerated by the Spirit, we may more and more withdraw ourselves from our own will and our own spirit, and so submit ourselves to thee, that thy Spirit may truly reign within us: And afterwards, grant that we may not be ungrateful, but considering how inestimable is this benefit, may we dedicate our whole life and apply ourselves to glorify thy name, in Jesus Christ our Lord. -- Amen

Ezekiel 11:22-23 – 12:7

Grant, Almighty God, since thou so wishest us to live in this world, that we may travel onwards till thou gatherest us into thy heavenly rest, that we may truly contemplate that eternal inheritance, and apply to it all our endeavors: and next, that we may so travel in this world that we may not wander nor stray from the way; but being always intent on the mark which thou settest before us, grant us to proceed on our way, until we finish our course, and enjoy that glory which thine only-begotten Son has prepared for us through his own blood. -- Amen

Ezekiel 12:8-16

Grant, Almighty God, since thou declarest to us by so many proofs the formidable nature of thine anger, especially against the obstinate and rebellious, who reject thy word familiarly spoken to them: Grant,

I say, that we may embrace what is proposed to us in thy name with the humility and reverence becoming' to thy children, so that we may repent of our sins, and obtain their pardon, until at length we are freed from all corruptions of the flesh, and become partakers of that eternal and celestial glory which thy only-begotten Son has purchased for us by his blood. -- Amen

Ezekiel 12:17-28

Grant us, Almighty God, since thou sparest us in some degree, and meanwhile dost admonish us by no obscure signs of thine anger, to be wise in time, lest sloth seize upon our minds and dispositions, and deprive us of sound judgment: Grant also that we may be attentive to thy words, and to all proofs of thy coming vengeance, and may we so strive to be reconciled to thee, that for the future being born again of thy Spirit, we may henceforth glorify thy name through Christ Jesus our Lord. -- Amen

Ezekiel 13:1-9

Grant, Almighty God, since we are so torpid in our vices that excitements are daily necessary to rouse us up, first, that our destined pastors may faithfully call us to repentance; then, that we in our turn may be so attentive to their exhortations, and so suffer ourselves to be condemned, that we may be our own judges: Grant also, that when you chastise us severely, the taste of thy paternal goodness may never be so lost to us, so that a way may always be open to us to seek reconciliation in Jesus Christ our Lord. -- Amen

Ezekiel 13:10-16

Grant, Almighty God, since we do not cease to provoke thee by our sins, that we may at length consider our wretched condition, unless you govern us by thy Spirit, and subject us to thyself in true obedience: and may we so desire to be reconciled to thee, that we may not flatter ourselves, but being altogether humbled and emptied of self, may we fly to thy mercy with a true feeling of piety: and so find what is prepared for us in Christ Jesus our Lord. -- Amen

Ezekiel 13:17-20

Grant, Almighty God, since you show us that our salvation is so precious in thy sight, that through our ingratitude we may not cast away this testimony of thy favor, but be anxious to listen to thy instructions: Grant also, that being gifted by thee with the spirit of discretion, we may not be exposed to capture as a prey; but may we be so ruled by the light of thy word that we may hold on in the right way, till after our allotted time is finished we may arrive at that happy repose which is laid up for us in heaven through Christ our Lord. -- Amen

Ezekiel 13:21-23 – 14:5

Grant, Almighty God, since we are so inclined to all kinds of vices, that we may be restrained by the power of thy Spirit: then that we may be attentive to the teaching which sounds continually in our ears, so that we may persevere in the pure worship of thy name; and thus being strengthened against the cunning of the wicked, may we be upheld in our weakness, and preserved from all error, until we finish our course, and arrive at the goal which is proposed to us in Christ Jesus our Lord. -- Amen

Ezekiel 14:6-9

Grant, Almighty God, since we are so prone to error, that thy truth may always shine upon us amidst the darkness of this world: Grant, also, that we may gaze upon it with open eyes, and subject ourselves to thee with true docility, so that being governed by both thy Word and thy Spirit, we may fulfill our course, and at length arrive at that happy rest, which your only begotten Son has prepared for us. Amen

Ezekiel 14:10-14

Grant, Almighty God, since you shine so clearly upon us with the teaching of thy Gospel, in which thy Son reveals himself familiarly to us, -- Grant that we may not shut our eyes to this light, or turn them hither and thither by depraved curiosity, but may remain in simple obedience, until at length having passed through the course of this life, we may arrive at the fullness of light, when you will transform us into thy glory by the same -- your only-begotten Son. -- Amen

Ezekiel 14:15-22

Grant, Almighty God, since you daily exercise thy judgments in all parts of the world, and since many regions are harassed by pestilence and war, that so long as you spare us we may profit by the evils and slaughters of others: Grant, also, if thy scourges reach also unto us, that we may not be obstinate, but may submit ourselves to thy judgment, and being truly humble, may we seek pardon by the serious pursuit of piety, so that we may truly acknowledge thee; and may feel thee to be a propitious Father to us, until at length we enjoy thy love in thy heavenly kingdom, through Christ our Lord. -- Amen

Ezekiel 14:23 – 15:1-8

Grant. Almighty God, since you have not only deigned to separate us from the common herd of men, but also to renew your image in us: and while thy favors towards us are conspicuous you exhort us at the same time to glorify thy name: Grant that being mindful of our calling we may study to devote ourselves wholly to thee and so to extol thee by peculiar and true and rightful praises, that we may be at length partakers of the glory to which you invite us, and which has been acquired for us by the blood of your only begotten Son. -- Amen

Ezekiel 16:1-8

Grant, Almighty God, since from our first origin we have been entirely accursed, so that we were entirely foul and polluted in thy sight, that we may be mindful of our condition, and acknowledge your inestimable pity towards us, since you have deigned to draw us from the lowest estate, and to adopt us among thy children: and may we so desire to spend our whole life in obedience to thee, that we may at length enjoy that blessed glory to which you has called us, and which you have prepared for us in your only-begotten Son. -- Amen

Ezekiel 16:9-16

Grant, Almighty God, that we may diligently consider in how many ways we are bound to thee, and may deservedly magnify thy fatherly indulgence towards us, so that in return we may desire to devote ourselves to thee: Grant also, that as you have adorned us with thy glory, we may endeavor to glorify thy name, until at length we arrive at the enjoyment of that eternal glory which you have prepared for us in heaven by Christ our Lord. -- Amen

Ezekiel 16:17-25

Grant, Almighty God, since you desire to receive us not only into confidence and dependence, but to the condition of sons, that we may worship thee with sacred love, and revere thee through our whole life as a Father; and may we so submit ourselves to thee as to feel thy covenant firm and sacred towards us; and may we experience that you never call men to thee in vain, so long as they obey thee and respond to thy promises; until at length we enjoy that blessedness which is laid up for us in heaven, through Christ our Lord. -- Amen

Ezekiel 16:26-32

Grant, Almighty God, since you have thought us worthy of such honor, that we should be bound to thee in your only-begotten Son by the bond of a spiritual marriage, -- that we may remain in that fidelity which we promised to thee, since we have found thee faithful to us by so many proofs on thy part, until, having passed through this present life, we arrive at the enjoyment of that blessedness which is the fruit of our faithful chastity, through Jesus Christ our Lord. -- Amen

Ezekiel 16:33-42

Grant, Almighty God, since you have hitherto sustained us, and since we are worthy of being utterly destroyed a hundred times, -- Grant, I say, that we may repent of ourselves, and prevent that horrible judgment of which you set before us a specimen in your ancient people: and may we so devote ourselves to thee in the true chastity of faith, that we may experience the course of thy goodness until we enjoy the eternal inheritance which your only-begotten Son has acquired for us by his blood. -- Amen

Ezekiel 16:43-49

Grant, Almighty God, since you have deigned to graft us once into the body of your only-begotten Son, that we may be mindful of our origin, since from our very birth we were lost and cursed; and grant that we may be mindful of that grace by which you have honored us, so that we may worship thee as a father, and preserve our trust in thee inviolate: and may we be so obedient to thee that thy image may be renewed in us more and more in all righteousness and holiness, until thy glory may perfectly shine forth in us in thy heavenly kingdom by the same Jesus Christ our Lord. -- Amen

Ezekiel 16:50-55

Grant, Almighty God, since in your inestimable mercy you have deigned to separate us from the profane nations, and to adopt us into thy family, that we may so conduct ourselves that you may not treat us as strangers: but while you acknowledge us as thy sons, may thy Spirit govern us until the end, so that thy name may be glorified in us, and at length we may be made partakers of that glory which has been acquired for us through Jesus Christ our Lord. -- Amen

Ezekiel 16:56-61

Grant, Almighty God, since your only-begotten Son has appeared for us, who filled up all the measure of thy grace, that we may not be ungrateful in despising so inestimable a boon; but may we embrace with true and sincere faith what you offer us, namely, the mercy which we always need, and also the spirit of regeneration; that we may so devote ourselves to thee through a whole life of obedience, that at length we may arrive at that glory which at this day: shines upon us as in a mirror, until its fruition shall appear in heaven, by the same Christ our Lord. -- Amen

Ezekiel 16:62-63 – 17:4

Grant, Almighty God, since you have treated us so liberally by opening the immense and inestimable treasures of thy grace, that being mindful of our condition we may always bewail it, and remember what we were when you desire to adopt us as sons, and how often and how variously we have provoked thee, and rendered thy covenant vain: Grant, also, that we may glorify thee in our shame, and perpetually magnify thy name by our humility, until we become partakers of that glory which your only-begotten Son has procured for us through his own blood. -- Amen

Ezekiel 17:5-16

Grant, Almighty God, since you show thy regard for mutual fidelity between man and man, that we may so conduct ourselves in every way that we may not deceive our brethren, but assist each other with sincere affection: Grant, also, that with true consent we may afford thee that confidence which you require, and which we are bound to pay thee; since you desire not only to enter into covenant with us by means of your only-be-gotten Son, but also to seal it with his blood, until we enjoy that inheritance which you have obtained for us by the sacrifice of his death. -- Amen

Ezekiel 17:17-23

Grant, Almighty God, since you have deigned to enter into a perpetual and inviolable covenant with us which you have sanctioned by the blood of your only-begotten Son, that we may faithfully stand to it: and may we be so obedient to thee unto the end, that we may experience thee a propitious Father to us, until we enjoy that eternal inheritance which you have prepared for us in heaven, through the same Christ our Lord.- Amen

Ezekiel 17:24 – 18:4

Grant, Almighty God, since you have not only created us out of nothing, but have deigned to create us again in your only-begotten Son, and have taken us from the lowest depths, and designed to raise us to the hope of thy heavenly kingdom: Grant, I say, that we may not be proud or puffed up with vainglory; but may we embrace this favor with becoming humility, and modestly submit ourselves to thee, until we become at length partakers of that glory which your only-begotten Son has acquired for us. -- Amen

Ezekiel 18:5-9

Grant, Almighty God, since you have so instructed us by thy law in the rules of living justly, that we have no excuse for error or ignorance: Grant, I say, that we may be attentive to that teaching which you prescribe for us; and so anxiously exercise ourselves in it, that each of us may live innocently among the brotherhood: and then may we so worship thee with one consent and so glorify thy name, that we may at length arrive at that happy inheritance which you have promised for us in your only-begotten Son. -- Amen

Ezekiel 18:10-17

Grant, Almighty God, since you have pointed out to us the true way of safety, since you did perceive us all deficient in this respect, and since the law which ought to have given us life brought death through our transgressing it: Grant, I pray thee, since you have set before us your only Son in whom we may be reconciled and obtain the perfect righteousness which we need, that we may so embrace the grace which is offered to us in the gospel, that we may strive more and more to proceed in the pursuit of piety, till we arrive at length at the blessed inheritance which the same, your only-begotten Son, has acquired for us. -- Amen

Ezekiel 18:18-23

Grant, Almighty God, since we are all lost in ourselves, that we may desire to obtain life where it is laid up for us, and where you do manifest it, namely, in thy Son: and grant that we may so embrace the grace which has been exhibited to us in the sacrifice of his death, that we may be regenerated by his Spirit; and thus being born again, may we devote ourselves wholly to thee, and so glorify thy name in this world, that we may at length be partakers of that glory which the same, your only-begotten Son, has acquired for us. -- Amen

Ezekiel 18:24-30

Grant, Almighty God, since nothing is more frail than we are, and even when you have once stretched forth your hand to us, we labor under such infirmity, that numberless falls await us unless you do succor us: Grant, I say, that being propped up by your unconquered strength, we may proceed in the course of thy holy calling, and may so bravely and perseveringly make war against all temptations, that we may at length enjoy in heaven the fruit of our victory, through Christ our Lord. -- Amen

Ezekiel 18:31-32 – 19:5

Grant, Almighty God, since we are all so depraved by nature that we are not only most deserving of being cast into the midst of lions, but are unworthy of being reckoned among thy creatures, that you may extend thy hand to us, and manifest thy wonderful power in reforming us; and may your image be so renewed in us, that we may daily make more and more progress in true piety and righteousness, until at length all the corruption's of the flesh may be abolished, and we may be partakers of that eternal glory which your only-begotten Son has acquired for us. -- Amen

Ezekiel 19:6-14

Grant, Almighty God, since you have once deigned to insert us into the body of thy Son, that we may be such vine-branches as you have undertaken to cultivate: that by the power of thy Spirit we may be so watered as never to be deficient in spiritual rigor: and may we so bear fruit to the glory of thy name, that we may at length arrive at the fountain of our faith when we enjoy the celestial glory to which you have adopted us in the name of your only-begotten Son, Jesus. Amen

Ezekiel 20:1-8

Grant, Almighty God, since you have once stretched forth your hand to us by your only-begotten Son, and have not only bound thyself to us by an oath, but have sealed your eternal covenant by the blood of the same, thy Son: Grant, I pray thee, that we in return may be faithful to thee, and persevere in the pure worship of thy name, until at length we enjoy the fruit of our faith in thy heavenly kingdom by the same Christ our Lord. -- Amen

Ezekiel 20:9-12

Grant, Almighty God, since you have not only deigned to bestow upon us a rule for living rightly, but has so shown thyself our Father in Christ as to be prepared to engrave thy law in our inward parts: Grant, I pray thee, that we may not cast away that inestimable boon through either ingratitude or sloth; but may we offer up ourselves to thee as a sacrifice: and then do you so pardon us that our infirmities may not hinder us from finding thee always propitious whenever we fly to thy mercy in Christ, your only-begotten Son. -- Amen

Ezekiel 20:13-20

Grant, Almighty God, since the doctrine of thy Gospel sounds daily in our ears, when you invite us so kindly by thy amazing clemency, and stretch out your hand by your only-begotten Son, -- Grant, I pray thee, that we may be of a teachable and flexible disposition, and that we may sincerely submit to thee: and since thy law contains so many dreadful examples of thy wrath, may we be moved by them, and may we walk with fear and trembling in obedience to thy word, that at length we may enjoy that inheritance which you have promised for us in thy heavenly kingdom, by the same Christ our Lord. -- Amen

Ezekiel 20:21-31

Grant, Almighty God, since you do not cease thy daily exhortations to repentance, but indulge us, and bear with us, while you correct us by thy word and thy chastisements, that we may not remain obstinate, but may learn to submit ourselves to thee: Grant, I pray thee, that we may not offer ourselves as thy disciples with feigned repentance, but be so sincerely and cordially devoted to thee, that we may desire nothing else than to progress more and more in the knowledge of thy heavenly doctrine, till at length we enjoy that full light which we hope for through our Lord Jesus Christ. -- Amen

Ezekiel 20:32-39

Grant, Almighty God, since you have once redeemed us by the death of your only-begotten Son, that we may not interrupt the course of thy favor by our ingratitude; but may we so proceed in obedience to thy Gospel, that we may be brought at length to the perfection of that grace which is commenced within us, and may proceed more and more every day in true piety, till at length we are gathered into thy heavenly kingdom, and enjoy the inheritance promised and obtained for us by the same Christ our Lord. -- Amen

Ezekiel 20:40-49

Grant, Almighty God, since we have already entered in hope upon the threshold of our eternal inheritance, and know that there is a certain mansion for us in heaven after Christ has been received there, who is our head, and the first-fruits of our salvation: Grant, I say, that we may proceed more and more in the course of thy holy calling until at length we reach the goal, and so enjoy that eternal glory of which you afford us a taste in this world, by the same Christ our

Lord. -- Amen

PRAISE TO GOD.

After finishing this last Lecture, that most illustrious man, John Calvin, the Divine, who had previously been sick, then began to be so much weaker that he was compelled to recline on a couch, and could no longer proceed with the explanation of Ezekiel. This accounts for his stopping at the close of the Twentieth Chapter, and not finishing the work so auspiciously begun. Nothing remains, kind Reader, but that you receive most favorably and graciously what is now sent forth to the world.

DANIEL

Daniel 1:1-3

Grant, Almighty God, since thou settest before us so clear a mirror of thy wonderful providence and of thy judgments on thine ancient people, that we may also be surely persuaded of our being under thy hand and protection - Grant, that relying on thee, we may hope for thy guardianship, whatever may happen, since thou never losest sight of our safety, so that we may invoke thee with a secure and tranquil mind. May we so fearlessly wait for all dangers amidst all the changes of this world, that we may stand upon the foundation of thy word which never can fail; and leaning on thy promises may we repose on Christ, to whom thou hast committed us, and whom thou hast made the shepherd of all thy flock. Grant that he may be so careful of us as to lead us through this course of warfare, however troublesome and turbulent it may prove, until we arrive at that heavenly rest which he has purchased for us by his own blood. Amen

Daniel 1:4-8

Grant, Almighty God, as long as our pilgrimage in this world continues, that we may feed on such diet for the necessities of the flesh as may never corrupt us; and may we never be led aside from sobriety, but may we learn to use our abundance by preferring abstinence in the midst of plenty. Grant also, that we may patiently endure want and famine, and eat and drink with such liberty as always to set before us the glory of thy Name. Lastly, may our very frugality lead us to aspire after that fullness by which we shall be completely refreshed, when the glory of thy countenance shall appear to us in heaven, through Jesus Christ our Lord. Amen

Daniel 1:9-16

Grant, Almighty God, since we are now encompassed by so many enemies, and the devil does not cease to harass us with fresh snares, so that the whole world is hostile to us, that we may perceive even the devil himself to be restrained by thy bridle. Grant, also, that all the impious may be subjected to thee, that thou mayest lead them whithersoever thou wishest. Do thou direct their hearts, and may we be experimentally taught how safe and secure we are under the protection of thy hand. And may we proceed, according to thy promise, in the course of our calling, until at length we arrive at that blessed rest which is laid up for us in heaven by Christ our Lord. Amen

Daniel 1:17 – 2:2

Grant, Almighty God, since every perfect gift comes from thee, and since some excel others in intelligence and talents, yet as no one has anything of his own, but as thou deignest to distribute to man a measure of thy gracious liberality, - Grant that whatever intelligence thou dost confer upon us, we may apply it to the glory of thy name. Grant also, that we may acknowledge in humility and modesty what thou hast committed to our care to be thine own; and may we study to be restrained by sobriety, to desire nothing superfluous, never to corrupt true and genuine knowledge, and to remain in that simplicity to which thou callest us. Finally, may we not rest in these earthly things, but learn rather to raise our minds to true wisdom, to acknowledge thee to be the true God, and to devote ourselves to the obedience of thy righteousness; and may it be our sole object to devote and consecrate ourselves entirely to the glory of thy name throughout our lives, through Jesus Christ our Lord. Amen

Daniel 2:3-9

Grant, Almighty God, since during our pilgrimage in this world we have daily need of the teaching and government of thy Spirit, that with true modesty we may depend on thy word and secret inspiration, and not take too much on ourselves, - Grant, also, that we may be conscious of our ignorance, blindness, and stupidity, and always flee, to thee, and never permit ourselves to be drawn aside in any way by the cunning of Satan and of the ungodly. May we remain so fixed in thy truth as never to turn aside from it, whilst thou dost direct us through the whole course of our vocation, and then may we arrive at that heavenly glory which has been obtained for us through the blood of thine only begotten Son. Amen

Daniel 2:10-19

Grant, Almighty God, since we are in danger every day and ever, moment, not merely from the cruelty of a single tyrant, but from the devil, who excites the whole world against us, arming the princes of this world, and impelling them to destroy us, - Grant, I pray thee, that we may feel and demonstrate, by experience, that our life is in thy hand, and that under thy faithful guardianship thou wilt not suffer one hair of our heads to fall. Do thou also so defend us, that the impious themselves may acknowledge that we do not boast this day in vain in thy name, nor invoke thee without success. And when we have experienced thy paternal anxiety, through the whole course of our life, may we arrive at that blessed immortality which thou hast promised us, and which is laid up for us in heaven, through Jesus Christ our Lord. Amen

Daniel 2:20-23

Grant, Almighty God, since we have so many testimonies to thy glory daily before our eyes, though we seem so blind as to shut out all the light by our ingratitude; grant, I pray, that we may at length learn to open our eyes; yea, do thou open them by thy Spirit. May we reflect on the number, magnitude, and importance of thy benefits towards us; and while thou dost set before us the proof of thy eternal divinity, grant that we may become proficient in this school of piety.

May we learn to ascribe to thee the praise of all. virtues, till nothing remains but to extol thee alone. And the more thou deignest to declare thyself liberal towards us, may we the more ardently desire to worship thee. May we devote ourselves to thee without reserving the slightest self praise, but caring for this only, that thy glory may remain and shine forth throughout all the world, through Christ our Lord. Amen

Daniel 2:24-30

Grant, Almighty God, since thou desirest us to differ from the brutes, and hence didst impress our minds with the light of intellect, - Grant, I pray thee, that we may learn to acknowledge and to magnify this singular favor, and may we exercise ourselves in the knowledge of those things which induce us to reverence thy sovereignty. Besides this, may we distinguish between that common sense which thou hast bestowed upon us, and the illumination of thy Spirit, and the gift of faith, that thou alone mayest be glorified by our being grafted by faith into the body of thine only-begotten Son. We entreat also from thee further progress and increase of the same faith, until at length thou bring us to the full manifestation of light. Then, being like thee, we shall behold thy glory face to face, and enjoy the same in Christ our Lord. Amen

Daniel 2:31-35

Grant, Almighty God, since we so travel through this world that our attention is easily arrested, and our judgment darkened, when we behold the power of the impious refulgent and terrible to ourselves and others. Grant, I say, that we may raise our eyes upwards, and consider how much power thou hast conferred upon thine only-begotten Son. Grant, also, that he may rule and govern us by the might of his Spirit, protect us by his faithfulness and guardianship, and compel the whole world to promote our salvation; thus may we rest calmly under his protection, and fight with that boldness and patience which he both commands and commends, until at length we enjoy the fruit of the victory which thou hast promised, and which thou wilt provide for us in thy heavenly kingdom. Amen

Daniel 2:36-43

Grant, Almighty God, that we may remember ourselves to be pilgrims in the world, and that no splendor of wealth, or power, or worldly wisdom may blind our eyes, but may we always direct our eyes and all our senses towards the kingdom of thy Son. May we always fix them there, and may nothing hinder us from hastening on in the course of our calling, until at length we pass over the course and reach the goal which thou hast set before us, and to which thou dost this day invite us by the heralding of thy gospel. Do thou at length gather us unto that happy eternity which has been obtained for us through the blood of the same, thy Son. May we never be separated from him, but, being sustained by his power, may we at last be raised by him to the highest heavens. Amen

Daniel 2:44-46

Grant, Almighty God, since thou hast shewn us by so many, such clear and such solid testimonies, that we can hope for no other Redeemer than him whom thou hast set forth and as thou hast sanctioned his divine and eternal power by so many miracles, and hast sealed it by both the preaching of the Gospel and the seal of thy Spirit in our hearts, and dost confirm the same by daily experience, - Grant that we may remain firm and stable in him. May we never decline from him may our faith never waver, but withstand all the temptations of Satan and may we so persevere in the course of thy holy calling, that we may be gathered at length unto that eternal blessedness and perpetual rest which has been obtained for us by the blood of the same, thy Son Amen

Daniel 2:47 – 3:1

Grant, Almighty God, since our minds have so many hidden recesses that nothing is more difficult than thoroughly to purge them from all fiction and lying, - Grant, I say, that we may honestly examine ourselves. Do thou also shine upon us with the light of thy Holy Spirit; may we truly acknowledge our hidden faults and put them far away from us, that thou mayest be our only God, and our true piety may obtain the palm of thine approbation. May we offer thee pure and spotless; worship, and meanwhile may we conduct ourselves in the world with a pure conscience; and may each of us be so occupied in our duties as to consult our brother's advantage as well as our own, and at length be made partakers of that true glory which thou hast prepared for us in heaven through Christ our Lord. Amen

Daniel 3:2-7

Grant, Almighty God, since we always wander miserably in our thoughts, and in our attempts to worship thee we only profane the true and pure reverence of thy Divinity, and are easily drawn aside to depraved superstition, - Grant that we may remain in pure obedience to thy word, and never bend aside from it in any way. Instruct us by the unconquered fortitude of thy Spirit. May we never yield to any terrors or threats of man, but persevere in reverencing thy name even to the end. However the world may rage after its own diabolic errors, may we never turn out of the right path, but continue in the right course in which thou invitees us, until, after finishing our race, we arrive at that happy rest which is laid up for us in heaven, through Christ our Lord. Amen

Daniel 3:8-18

Grant, Almighty God, since we see the impious carried away by their impure desires with so strong an impulse; and while they are so puffed up with arrogance, may we learn true humility, and so subject ourselves to thee that we may always depend upon thy word and always attend to thy instructions. When we have learned what worship pleases thee, may we constantly persist unto the end, and never be moved by any threats, or dangers, or violence, from our position, nor drawn aside from our course; but by persevering: obedience to thy word, may we shew our alacrity and obedience, until thou dost acknowledge us as thy sons, and we are gathered to that eternal inheritance which thou hast prepared for all members of Christ thy Son. Amen

Daniel 3:19-20

Grant, Almighty God, since our life is only for a moment, nay, is only vanity and smoke, that we may learn to cast all our care upon thee, and so to depend upon thee, as not to doubt time as our deliverer from all urgent perils, whenever it shall be to our advantage. Grant us also to learn to neglect and despise our lives, especially for the testimony of thy glory; and may we be prepared to depart as soon as thou callest us from this world. May the hope of eternal life be so fixed in our hearts, that we may willingly leave this world and aspire with all our mind towards that blessed eternity which thou hast testified to be laid up for us in heaven, through the gospel, and which thine only-begotten Son has procured for us through his blood. Amen

Daniel 3:26

Grant, Almighty God, since thou hast instructed us by the doctrine of thy law and Gospel, and dost daily deign to make known thy will to us with familiarity, that we may remain fixed in the true obedience of this teaching, in which thy perfect justice is manifested; and may we never be moved away from thy worship. May we be prepared, whatever happens, rather to undergo a hundred deaths than to turn aside from the profession of true piety, in which we know our safety to be laid up. And may we so glorify thy name as to be partakers of that glory which has been acquired for us through the blood of thine only-begotten Son. Amen

Daniel 4:1-9

Grant, Almighty God, since thou here proposest a remarkable example before our eyes, that we may learn thy power to be so great as not to be sufficiently celebrated by any human praises: and since we hear how its herald was a profane king, nay, even a. cruel and proud one, and thou hast afterwards deigned to manifest thyself to us familiarly in Christ, - Grant, that in the spirit. of humility we may desire to glorify thee, and to cleave entirely to thee. May we declare thee to be ours, not only in mouth and tongue, but also in works; not only as our true and only God, but our Father, since thou hast adopted us in thine only-begotten Son, until at length we enjoy that eternal inheritance which is laid up for us in heaven by the same Christ our Lord. Amen

Daniel 4:10-16

Grant, Almighty God, since we see it so difficult for us. to bear prosperity without injury to the mind, that we may remember ourselves to be mortal - may our frailty be ever present to our eyes, and tender us humble, and lead us to ascribe the glory to thee. Being advised by thee, may we learn to walk with anxiety and fear, to submit ourselves to thee, and to conduct ourselves modestly towards our brethren. May none of us despise or insult his brother, but may we all strive to discharge our duties with moderation, until at length thou gatherest us into that glory which has been obtained for us by the blood of thine only-begotten Son. Amen

Daniel 4:1-24

Grant, Almighty God, since thou settest before us our sins, and at the same time announcest thyself as our judge, that we may not abuse thy forbearance and lay up for ourselves a treasure of greater wrath through our sloth and torpor. Grant, also, that we may fear thee reverently, and be anxiously cautious ourselves: may we be frightened by thy threats, and enticed by thy sweetness, and be willing and submissive to thee: may we never desire more than to consecrate ourselves entirely to obey thee, and to glorify thy name through Jesus Christ our Lord. Amen

Daniel 4:25-27

Grant, Almighty God, that we may learn to bear patiently all adverse misfortunes, and know that thou exercisest towards us the duties of a judge, as often as we are afflicted in this world. Thus may we prevent thy wrath, and so condemn ourselves with true humility, that trusting in thy pity we may always flee to thee, relying upon the mediation of thy only-begotten Son, which thou hast provided for us. Grant, also, that we may beg pardon of thee, and resolve upon a true repentance, not with vain and useless fictions, but by true and serious proofs, cultivating true charity and faith among ourselves, and testifying in this way our fear of thy name, that thou mayest be truly glorified in us by the same our Lord. Amen

Daniel 4:28-32-34

Grant, Almighty God, (since we are nothing in ourselves, and yet we cease not to please ourselves, and so are blinded by our vain confidence, and then we vainly boast in our virtues, which are worthless,) that we may learn to put off these perverse affections. May we so submit to thee as to depend upon thy mere favor: may we know ourselves, to stand and be sustained by thy strength alone: may we learn so to glorify thy name that we may not only obey thy word with true and pure humility, but also earnestly implore thy assistance, and distrusting ourselves, may rely upon thy favor as our only support, until at length thou gatherest us into thy heavenly kingdom, where we may enjoy that blessed eternity which has been obtained for us by thine only-begotten Son Amen

Daniel 4:35-37

Grant, Almighty God, since the disease of pride remains fixed in us all through our original corruption in our father Adam, - Grant, I say, that we may learn to mortify our spirits, and to be displeased with our conduct, as we ought; may we feel ourselves to be deprived of all wisdom and rectitude without thee alone. May we fly to thy pity, and confess ourselves utterly subject to eternal death; may we rely on thy goodness which thou hast deigned to offer us through thy Gospel; may we trust in that Mediator whom thou hast given us; may we never hesitate to fly to thee, to call upon thee as our Father, and having been renewed by thy Spirit, may we walk in true humility and modesty, till at length thou shalt raise us to that heavenly kingdom which has been obtained for us by the blood of thine only-begotten Son. Amen

Daniel 5:1-5

Grant, Almighty God, since we are so prone to forgetfulness and to our own indulgence in the desires and pleasures of the flesh, - Grant, I say, to each of us to be recalled to the contemplation of thy judgments; and may we be anxious to walk as in thy sight. May we be afraid of thy just vengeance, be careful not to provoke it by our petulance and other vices; but may we submit ourselves to thee, be held up, and propped up by thy hands, and proceed in the sacred course of thy calling, until at length thou shalt raise us to thy heavenly kingdom, which has been acquired for us by the blood of thine only-begotten Son. Amen

Daniel 5:6-11

Grant, Almighty God, since thou dost constantly address us by thy Prophets, and permittest us not to wander in the darkness of error, - Grant us, I say, to be attentive to thy voice, and make us docile and tractable towards thee; especially when thou settest before us a Master in whom are included all treasures of wisdom and knowledge. Grant us further, I pray thee, to be subject to thine only-begotten Son, to hold on in the right course of our holy calling, and to be always pressing onwards to that goal to which thou callest us, until we are successful in all our contests with this world, and at length arrive at that blessed rest which thou hast obtained for us through the blood of the same thy Son. Amen

Daniel 5:12-20

Grant, Almighty God, since our own station in life has been assigned to us, that we may be content with our lot, and when thou dost humble us, may we willingly be subject to thee, and suffer ourselves to be ruled by thee, and not desire any exaltation, which may lead us down to destruction. Grant us also, to conduct ourselves so modestly in our various callings, that thou mayest always shine forth in. us. May nothing else be set before us than to assist our brethren to whom we are attached, as in thy sight; and thus glorify thy name among all men, through Jesus Christ our Lord. Amen

Daniel 5:21-29

Grant, Almighty God, that as thou didst once send forth a proof of thy wrath against all the proud, so it may be useful to us in these days. May we be admonished by the punishment inflicted on this man, and thus learn to conduct ourselves with moderation and humility. May we not desire any greatness which can be displeasing to thee; and may we so remain in our station of life as to serve thee, and to extol and glorify thy sacred name, without being even separated from thee. Grant us also so to bear thy yoke in this world, and to suffer ourselves to be ruled by thee, that we may at length arrive at that happy rest and portion in thy heavenly kingdom, which thou hast prepared and procured for us, through the blood of thine only-begotten Son. Amen

Daniel 5:30-31 – 6:7

Grant, Almighty God, as thou didst govern thy servant Daniel when honors were flowing around on all sides, and he was raised to the highest dignity, and preserve him safe in his integrity and innocency amidst the universal licentiousness, - Grant, I pray thee, that we may learn to restrain ourselves within that moderation to which thou restrictest us. May we be content with our humble station and strive to prove ourselves innocent before thee and before those with whom we have to deal; so that thy name may be glorified in us, and we may proceed under thy shelter against the malice of mankind. Whenever Satan besieges us on every side, and the wicked lay snares for us, and we are attacked by the fierceness of wild beasts, may we remain safe under thy protection, and even if we have to undergo a hundred deaths, may we learn to live and die to thee, and may thy name be glorified in us, through Christ our Lord. Amen

Daniel 6:8-9-12

Grant, Almighty God, since thou hast reconciled us to thyself by the precious blood of thy Son, that we may not be our own, but devoted to thee in perfect obedience, and may consecrate ourselves entirely to thee: May we offer our bodies and souls in sacrifice, and be rather prepared to suffer a hundred deaths than to decline from thy true and sincere worship. Grant us, especially, to exercise ourselves in prayer, to fly to thee every moment, and to commit ourselves to thy Fatherly care, that thy Spirit may govern us to the end. Do thou defend and sustain us, until we are collected into that heavenly kingdom which thy only-begotten Son has prepared for us by his blood. Amen

Daniel 6:13-20

Grant, Almighty Father, since thou shewest us, by the example of thy servant Daniel, how we ought to persevere with consistency in the sincere worship of thee, and thus proceed towards true greatness of mind, that we may truly devote ourselves to thee. May we not be turned aside in any direction through the lust of men, but may we persist in our holy calling, and so conquer all dangers, and arrive at length at the fruit of victory - that happy immortality which is laid up for us in heaven, through Christ our Lord. Amen

Daniel 6:21-24

Grant, Almighty God, since we were created and placed in this world by thee, and are also nourished by thy bounty, for the very purpose of consecrating our life to thee, - Grant, I pray, that we may be prepared to live and die to thee. May we seek only to maintain the pure and sincere worship of thyself. May we so acquiesce in thy help as not to hesitate about breaking through all difficulties, and to offer ourselves to instant death, whenever thou requirest it. May we rely not only on thy promise, which remains for ever, but upon the many proofs which thou hast granted us of the present vitality of thy mighty power. Mayest thou be our deliverer in every sense, whether we live or die; and may we be blessed in persevering in our confidence in thy name, and thy true confession, until at length we are gathered into thy heavenly kingdom, which thou hast prepared for us by the blood of thine only-begotten Son. Amen

Daniel 6:25-28

Grant, Almighty God, since by means of a man entangled in many errors, thou wishest to testify to us the extent of thy power, that we may not at this day grope about in darkness, while thou offerest us light, through the Sun of righteousness, Jesus Christ, thy Son. Meanwhile, may we not be ashamed to profit by the words of a heathen, who was not instructed in thy law, but who celebrated thy name so magnificently when admonished by a single miracle: hence may we learn by his example to acknowledge thee, not only the Supreme but the Only God. As thou hast bound us to thyself by entering into a covenant with us in the blood of thine only-begotten Son, may we ever cleave to thee with true faith; may we renounce all the clouds of error, and be always intent upon that light to which thou invitest us, and towards which thou drawest us; until we arrive at the sight of thy glory and majesty, and being conformed to thee, may we at length enjoy in reality that glory which we now but partially behold. Amen

Daniel 7:1-5

Grant, Almighty God, since thou exposest us to various distresses in this world, for the purpose of exercising our faith and patience: Grant, I say, that we may remain tranquil in our station, through reliance on thy promises. When storms gather around us on all sides, may we never fall away and never despond in our courage, but persevere in our calling. Whatever may happen, may we recognize thee as carrying on the government of the world, not only to punish the ingratitude of the reprobate, but to retain thine own people in thy faith and protection, and preserve them to the end. May we bear patiently whatever changes may happen to us and may we never be disturbed or distressed in our minds, till at length we are gathered into that happy rest, where we shall be free from all warfare and all contests, and enjoy that eternal blessness which thou hast prepared for us in thine only begotten Son. Amen

Daniel 7:6-8

Grant, Almighty God, since thou hast formerly admonished thy servants, that thy children, while they are pilgrims in this world, must be familiar with horrible and cruel beasts, if the same thing should happen to us, that we may be prepared for all contests. May we endure and overcome all temptations, and may we never doubt thy desire to defend us by thy protection and power, according to thy promise. May we proceed through the midst of numberless dangers, until after accomplishing the course of our warfare, we at length arrive at that happy rest which is laid up for us in heaven by Christ our Lord. Amen

Daniel 7:9-11

Grant, Almighty God, whatever revolutions happen daily in the world, that we may always be intent on the sight of thy glory, once manifested to us in thy Son. May the splendor of thy majesty illuminate our hearts, and may we pass beyond the visible heavens, the sun, the moon, and every shining thing; and may we behold the blessedness of thy kingdom, which thou proposest to us in the light of thy Gospel. May we walk through the midst of the darkness and afflictions of the world, content with that light by which thou invitest us to the hope of the eternal inheritance which thou hast promised us, and acquired for us by the blood of thine only begotten Son. Amen

Daniel 7:12-16

Grant, Almighty God, since the faith of the fathers was supported by obscure shadows, by which thou didst wish it to be nourished, until thy Son was manifestly revealed to us in the flesh: Grant, I pray thee, at this day, after he has appeared to us as the best and most perfect teacher, and explained thy counsels to us similarly, that we may not be either so dull or so careless as to allow the great clearness of the manifestation of thyself offered us in the Gospel to escape from our grasp. May we be so directed towards life eternal, until after the performance of our course in this present life, and the removal of all obstacles which Satan places in our way, either to delay us or turn us aside, we may at length arrive at the enjoyment of that blessed life in which Christ., thine only begotten Son, has preceded us. May we thus be co-heirs with him, and as thou hast appointed him sole inheritor, so may he gather us unto the secure inheritance of a blessed immortality. Amen

Daniel 7:17-22

Grant, Almighty God, since thou profest our faith and constancy by many trials, as it is our duty in this respect and in all others, to submit to thy will: Grant, I pray, that we may not give way to the many attacks by which we are tossed about. For we are assailed on all sides by Satan and all the impious, and while their fury is ever burning and raging cruelly against us, may we never yield to it. May we proceed in our warfare, in reliance on the unconquered might of the Spirit, even though impious men prevail for a season. May we look forward to the advent of thy only-begotten Son, not only when he shall appear at the last day, but also whenever it shall please time for him to assist thy Church, and to raise it out of its miserable afflictions. And even if we must endure our distresses, may our courage never fail us, until at length we are gathered into that holy rest, which has been obtained for us through the blood of the same, thine only-begotten Son Amen

Daniel 7:23-25

Grant, Almighty God, since we must be daily exercised by various contests, that we may never yield to the infirmities of the flesh, and never forget thy Holy calling. Animate us, we pray thee, for all hostile engagements; may we stand unbroken against all the assaults of Satan and the wicked; and thus give ourselves up and devote ourselves to thee. May we never hesitate to suffer death itself, if necessary, and even to offer ourselves daily to various kinds of death, until we shall have discharged our warfare, and enjoy that happy and eternal rest which thou hast prepared for us in thine only-begotten Son. Amen

Daniel 7:26-28

Grant, Almighty God, since thou formerly didst permit thy servants to maintain their courage in the midst of so many and such heavy commotion, that we may reap the same edification from these prophecies: are since we have fallen upon the fullness of times, may we profit by the examples of the ancient Church, and by the pious and holy admonitions which thou hast set before us. Thus may we stand firm and unconquered against all the attacks of Satan, and the world, and the impious, and so may our faith remain impregnable, until at length we enjoy the fruit of its victory in thy heavenly kingdom, through Christ our Lord. Amen

Daniel 8:1-7

Grant, Almighty God, since thou desirest us to be tossed about amidst many and various convulsions, that our minds may always look upwards towards heaven, where thou hast prepared for us certain rest and a tranquil inheritance beyond the reach of disturbance and commotion. When the land through which we are on pilgrimage is in confusion, may we be so occupied during its storms, as to stand composed and grounded upon the faith of thy promises, until having discharged our warfare, we are gathered together into that happy rest, where we shall enjoy the fruit of our victory, in

Christ Jesus our Lord. Amen

Daniel 8:8-12

Grant, Almighty God, as thou hast enlightened us by the teaching of thy Gospel, and set before our eyes thine only begotten Son as a Sun of righteousness to rule us, and hast deigned to separate us from the whole world, and to make us thy peculiar people, and to prepare for us a certain seat in heaven: Grant, I pray thee, that we may be heirs of eternal life. Grant us also, to be mindful of thy sacred calling, and to make our pilgrimage on earth with spirits looking upwards and tending towards thee. May we meditate upon the righteousness of thy kingdom, and be entirely devoted to thee. Do thou protect us by thy hand even to the end, and may we march boldly under thy standard, till at length we arrive at that blessed rest, where the fruit of our victory is laid up for us in Jesus Christ our Lord. Amen

Daniel 8:13-16

Grant, Almighty God, since in these days the earth is full of defilement's which pollute the sacred worship of thy name, as there is scarcely a corner of the world which Satan has not corrupted, and as thy truth is everywhere adulterated, that we may persevere and remain steadfast in our course of piety. May we always be attentive to that light which thou didst first set before us in the Law, and which shines upon us now more fully under the Gospel. May we never become plunged into that darkness in which we see the world wrapped up, and in which those who seem to be themselves most acute are still involved. Grant us always to follow that life which thou shewest us, until we arrive at that goal which thou hast set before us, and to which thou daily invitest us by thine only-begotten Son. Amen

Daniel 8:17-25

Grant, Almighty God, since we see thy Church throughout all ages to have been exercised by the Cross in various ways, and with constant suffering, that we also may prepare ourselves for undergoing whatever thou mayest lay upon us. May we learn also to consider our sins as the cause of whatever adversity happens to us; may we consider thee to be not only faithful in all thy promises, but also a Father - propitious to those wretched ones who suppliantly fly to thee for pardon. When we are humbled under thy powerful hand, may we be raised up by the hope of eternal salvation which is prepared for us. Thus may we look for a happy and joyful termination of all our contests, until we enjoy the fruit of our victory in thy' heavenly kingdom, as it has been obtained for us by the blood of thine only-begotten Son. Amen

Daniel 8:26-27

Grant, Almighty God, as in these days thou hast called us to a similar lot to that which the fathers under the Law formerly experienced, and as thou didst confirm them in patience, and arm them for constancy in warfare, and render them superior in all conflicts with Satan and the world. Grant, I pray thee, that we at this day, whom thou wishest to be joined to them, may become proficient in thy word. May we look forward to bearing the cross throughout our whole life. May we be prepared for the contest, and prefer miserable affliction under the standard of the cross, to spending a secure and luxurious life in our own enjoyments, and thus becoming deprived of that hope of victory which thou hast promised us, and whose fruit thou hast laid up for us in heaven, through Jesus Christ our Lord. Amen

Daniel 9:1-4

Grant, Almighty God, as at the present time thou dost deservedly chastise us for our sins, according to the example of thine ancient people, that we may turn our face to thee with true penitence and humility: May we throw ourselves suppliantly and prostrately before thee; and, despairing of ourselves, place our only hope in thy pity which thou hast promised us. May we rely on that adoption which is founded on and sanctioned by thine only-begotten Son, and never hesitate to come to thee as a father whenever we fly to thee. Meanwhile, do thou so thoroughly affect our minds, that we may not only pray to thee as a matter of duty, but truly and seriously take refuge in thee, and be touched with a sense of our sins, and never doubt thy propitious disposition towards us, in the name of the same thy Son our Lord. Amen

Daniel 9:5-7

Grant, Almighty God, as no other way of access to thee is open for us except through unfeigned humility, that we may often learn to abase ourselves with feelings of true repentance. May we be so displeased with ourselves as not to be satisfied with a single confession of our iniquities; but may we continue in the same state of meditation, and be more and more penetrated with real grief. Then may we fly to thy mercy, prostrate ourselves before thee in silence, and acknowledge no other hope but thy pity and the intercession of thine only-begotten Son. May we be so reconciled to thee, as not only to be absolved from our sins, but also governed throughout the whole course of our life by thy Holy Spirit, until at length we enjoy the victory in every kind of contest, and arrive at that blessed rest which thou hast prepared for us by the same our Lord Jesus Christ. Amen

Daniel 9:8-13

Grant, Almighty God, that we may learn seriously to consider in how many ways we become guilty before thee, especially while we daily continue to provoke thy wrath against us. May we be humbled by true and serious repentance, and fly eagerly to thee, as nothing is left to us but thy pity alone; when cast down and confounded, and reduced to nothing in ourselves, may we fly to this sacred anchor, as thou art easily entreated, and hast promised to act as a father of mercies to all sinners who seek thee. Thus may we approach thee with true penitence, and relying on thy goodness, never doubt the granting of our requests; and being freed by thy mercy from the tyranny of Satan and of sin, may we be governed by thy Holy Spirit, and so directed in the way of righteousness as to glorify thy name throughout our lives, till we arrive at that happy and immortal life which we know to be laid up in heaven for us, by Christ our Lord. Amen

Daniel 9:14-17

Grant, Almighty God, as thou hast deigned to gather us once among thy people, and hast wished us also to bear thy name, and that of thine only-begotten Son; although we so often provoke thine anger by our sins, and never cease to heap evil upon evil: Grant that we may never be exposed as a laughing-stock and spectacle, to the disgrace of thy sacred name. As, therefore, thou now seest the impious seizing all occasions of grossly slandering thyself, and thy sacred gospel, and the name of thine only-begotten Son, do not permit them, I pray thee, petulantly to insult thee. May thy Spirit so govern us, that we may desire to glorify thy name. May it be glorified in spite of Satan and all the impious, until we are gathered into that celestial kingdom which thou hast promised us in the same Christ our Lord.-Amen

Daniel 9:18-21

Grant, Almighty God, that we may learn more and more fully to probe ourselves, and to discover the faults of which we are guilty: nay, may the serious weight of our wickedness truly humble us when we come into thy sight, and call upon thee even from the lowest depths. May we never cease to hope for thy grace; may we be elevated by that hope to the highest heavens, and be firmly assured that thou wilt always prove thyself a propitious Father to us. And as thou hast granted us a Mediator who may procure favor for us from thee, may we never hesitate to approach thee familiarly, through reliance on him. Whenever our miseries induce us to despair, may we never succumb to it; but with unconquered fortitude of mind, may we persevere in invoking thy name and imploring thy pity, until we perceive the fruit of our prayers, and after being freed from all warfare, may we at length arrive at that blessed rest which is laid up for us in heaven, by the same, Christ our Lord. Amen

Daniel 9:22-24

Grant, Almighty God, as through our extreme blindness, we cannot gaze upon open daylight, that we may be enlightened by thy Spirit. May we profit by all thy prophecies by which thou wishest to direct us to thine only-begotten Son; embrace him with true and certain faith, and remain obedient to him as our ruler and guide; and after we have passed through this world, may we at length arrive at that heavenly rest which has been obtained for us by the blood of the same thy Son. Amen

Daniel 9:25

Grant, Almighty God, since thy servants before the setting forth of thine only-begotten Son were sustained by those oracles which had not then been realized by the event, that we at; this day may learn to put our trust in our Lord, who has so clearly revealed himself to us by his Gospel. May we stand so firm and constant in the faith of that Gospel, that we may never be tossed about by the disturbances and tumults of this world. May we ever proceed in the course of thy holy calling, till at length we are released from all contests, and arrive at that blessed rest which is laid up for us in heaven, by the same our Lord Jesus Christ. Amen

Daniel 9:26-27

Grant, Almighty God, since all the treasures of thy goodness and indulgence were so liberally diffused, when thine only-begotten Son appeared, and are now daily offered to us through the Gospel: Grant, I say, that we may not deprive ourselves of such important blessings by our ingratitude. May we embrace thy Son with true faith; and enjoy the benefit of the redemption which he has procured for us. Being cleansed and purged by his blood, may we be acceptable in thy sight, and venture with full and certain confidence to call thee Father. May we fly to thy pity and assistance in all our miseries and troubles, until at length thou shalt gather us into that eternal rest, which has been obtained for us through the blood of thine only-begotten Son. Amen

Daniel 10:1-3

Grant, Almighty God, since thou settest before us so remarkable an example in thy holy Prophet, whom thou didst adorn in so many ways that he wrestled to even extreme old age with various and almost innumerable trials, and yet was never mentally broken down: Grant us to be endowed with the same untiring fortitude. May we proceed in the course of our holy calling without the slightest despondency through whatever may happen. When we see thy Church upon the brink of ruin, and its enemies plotting desperately for its destruction, may we constantly look for that liberty which thou hast promised. May we strive with unbroken courage, until at length we shall be discharged from our warfare, and gathered into that blessed rest which we know to be laid up for us in heaven, through Christ our Lord. Amen

Daniel 10:4-8

Grant, Almighty God, as thou didst formerly appear to Daniel thy holy servant, and to the other prophets, and by their doctrine didst render thy glory conspicuous to us at this day, that we may reverently approach and behold it. When we have become entirely devoted to thee, may those mysteries which it has pleased thee to offer by means of their hand and labors, receive from us their due estimation. May we be cast down in ourselves and be raised by hope and faith towards heaven; when prostrate before thy face, may we so conduct ourselves in the world, as in the interval to become free from all the depraved desires and passions of our flesh, and dwell mentally in heaven. Then at length may we be withdrawn from this earthly warfare, and arrive at that celestial rest which thou hast prepared for us, through the same Jesus Christ our Lord. Amen

Daniel 10:9-14

Grant, Almighty God, as the weakness of our faith is such that it almost vanishes on the very least occasion: Grant, I say, that we may not hesitate to derive support from this remarkable and memorable example which thou wishest to propose to us in Daniel, although for a time thou hidest thy face from us, and we lie prostrate in darkness. Still do thou remain near us; and with undoubting hope may we be steadfast in our prayers and groaning, until at length the fruit of our prayers shall appear. Thus may we constantly make war with all kinds of trials, and persist unconquered until thou shalt stretch forth thine hand from heaven to us, and raise us to that blessed rest which is there laid up for us by Christ our Lord. Amen

Daniel 10:15-21

Grant, Almighty God, as thou daily and familiarly deignest to grant us the light of heavenly doctrine, that we may come to thy school with true humility and modesty. May our docility be really apparent; may we receive with reverence whatever proceeds from thy lips, and may thy majesty be conspicuous among us. May we taste of that goodness which thou dost manifest to us in thy word, and be enabled to rejoice in thee as our Father; may we never dread thy presence, but may we enjoy the sweet testimony of thy paternal grace and favor. May thy word be more precious to us than gold and worldly treasures, and, meanwhile, may we feed upon its sweetness, until we arrive all that full satiety which is laid up for us in heaven through Christ our Lord. Amen

Daniel 11:1-5

Grant, Almighty God, since thou not only deignedst to unfold future events to thy servant Daniel, and to the pious who waited for the advent of thine only-begotten Son, that they might be prepared for all sufferings, and might perceive the Church to repose under thy care and protection, but also wishedst these prophecies to profit us at this day, and to confirm us in the same doctrine: Grant us to learn how to cast all our cares and anxieties on thy paternal providence. May we never doubt thy oversight of the cares of thy Church in these days, and thy protection against the fury of the ungodly who try all means of destroying it. May we repose in peace under that guardianship which thou hast promised us, and struggle on under the standard of the cross; and possess our souls in patience, until at length thou shalt appear as our Redeemer with outstretched hand, at the manifestation of thy Son, when he returns to judge the world. Amen

Daniel 11:6-11

Grant, Almighty God, as thou hast deigned to set before our eyes as in a glass that peculiar providence of thine by which thou defendest thy Church: Grant, that being confirmed by these examples, we may learn to repose entirely upon thee. Amidst the numerous disturbances by which the world is at this time agitated, may we remain quiet under thy protection. May we so commit our safety to thee as never to hesitate, whatever may happen, as to our future safety and security. Whatever we may suffer, may it all issue in our salvation, while we are protected by thy hand; thus will we call upon thy name with sincerity of mind, and thou wilt in return shew thyself as our Father in thine only-begotten Son. Amen

Daniel 11:12-18

Grant, Almighty God, since it pleases thee to exercise our confidence by not allowing us any fixed or stable rest upon earth, that we may learn to rest in thee while the world rolls over and over even a hundred times. May we never doubt either our protection under thy hand, or the perpetual issue of all things in our good. Although we are not beyond the reach of darts, yet may we know the impossibility of our suffering under any deadly wound, when thou puttest forth thy hand to shield us. May we have full confidence in thee, and never cease to march under thy standard with constant and invincible courage, until at length thou shalt gather us into that happy rest which is laid up for us in heaven, by Christ our Lord. Amen

Daniel 11:19-25

Grant, Almighty God, that we may remain quiet under thy shelter and protection, hi the midst of those numerous disturbances which thou ever submittest to our eyes in this world. May we never lose our courage when an occasion is given to Satan and our enemies to oppress us, but may we remain secure trader thy protection, and every hour and every moment may we fly to thy guardianship. Relying on thine unconquered power, may we never hesitate so to pass through all commotion's, as to repose with quiet minds upon thy grace, till at length we are gathered into that happy and eternal rest which thou hast prepared for us in heaven, by Jesus Christ our Lord. Amen

Daniel 11:26-32

Grant, Almighty God, that as we are instructed by thy Spirit and armed by thy sacred teaching, we may carry on the war bravely with open enemies and with all who boldly oppose true religion. May we also constantly despise all domestic foes and apostates, and resist them manfully. May we never be disturbed, even if various tumults should arise in thy Church. May we fix our eyes upon thee, and always expect a happier issue than appears possible at the time, until at length thou shalt fulfill thy promises. And may all events which now seem contrary to us, issue in our salvation, when thy Son our Redeemer shall appear. Amen

Daniel 11:33-34

Grant, Almighty God, as at this day thou dost try the faith of thy people by many tests, that they may obtain strength from the unconquered fortitude of thy Holy Spirit. May we constantly march under thy standard, even to the end, and never succumb to any temptation. May we there join intelligence with zeal in building up thy Church: as each of us is endowed with superior gifts, so may he strive for the edification of his brethren with greater boldness, manliness, and fervor, while he endeavors to add numbers to the cause. And should the number of those who are professed members of thy Church diminish, yet may some seed always remain, until abundant produce shall flow forth from it, and such fruitfulness arise as shall cause thy name to be glorified throughout the whole world, in Jesus Christ our Lord. Amen

Daniel 11:35-36

Grant, Almighty God, as in these days the affairs of the world are in a state of disturbance, and as wherever we turn our eyes we see nothing but horrible confusion: Grant, I pray, that we may be attentive to thy teaching. May we never wander after our own imaginations, never be drawn aside by any cares, and never turn aside from our stated course. May we remain fixed in thy word, always seeking thee and always relying on thy providence. May we never hesitate concerning our safety, as thou hast undertaken to be the guardian of our salvation, but ever call upon thee in the name of thine only-begotten Son. Amen

Daniel 11:37-39

Grant, Almighty God, as in all ages the blindness of mankind has been so great as to lead them to worship thee erroneously and superstitiously, and since they manifest such duplicity and pride as to despise thy name, and also the very idols which they have fashioned for themselves: Grant, I pray thee, that true piety may be deeply rooted in our hearts. May the fear of thy name be so engraven within us, that we may be sincerely and unreservedly devoted to thee. May each of us heartily desire to glorify thy name, and may we endeavor to lead our brethren in the same course. Do thou purge us more and more from all dissimulation, until at length we arrive at that perfect purity which is laid up for us in heaven, through Jesus Christ our Lord. Amen

Daniel 11:40-45

Grant, Almighty God, since we are placed in similar distresses to those of which thou dost wish to warn us by thy angel, as well as thine ancient people, that thy light may shine upon us by means of thy only-begotten Son. May we feel ourselves always in safety under his invincible power. May we dwell securely under his shadow, and contend earnestly and boldly unto the end, against Satan and all his impious crew. And when all our warfare is over, may we arrive at last at that blessed rest where the fruit of our victory awaits us, in the same Christ our Lord. Amen

Daniel 12:1-4

Grant, Almighty God, as we have to engage in battle through the whole course of our lives, and our strength is liable to fail in various ways, that we may be supported by thy power and thus persevere unto the end. May we never grow weary, but learn to overcome the whole world, and to look forward to that happy eternity to which thou invitest us. May we never hesitate while Christ thy Son fights for us, in whose hand and power our victory is placed, and may he ever admit us into alliance with himself in that conquest which he has procured for us, until at length he shall gather us at the last day into the enjoyment of that triumph in which he has gone before us. Amen

Daniel 12:5-13

Grant, Almighty God, since thou proposest to us no other end than that of constant warfare during our whole life, and subjectest us to many cares until we arrive at the goal of this temporary race-course: Grant, I pray thee, that we may never grow fatigued. May we ever be armed and equipped for battle, and whatever the trials by which thou dost prove us, may we never be found deficient. May we always aspire towards heaven with upright souls, and strive with all our endeavors to attain that blessed rest which is laid up for us in heaven, in Jesus Christ our Lord. Amen

HOSEA

Hosea 1:1-2

Grant, Almighty God, that as thou hast once adopted us, and continues to confirm this thy favour by calling us unceasingly to thyself, and dost not only severely chastise us, but also gently and paternally invite us to thyself, and exhort us at the same time to repentance, - O grant that we may not be so hardened as to resist thy goodness, nor abuse this thine incredible forbearance, but submit ourselves in obedience to thee; that whenever thou mayest severely chastise us, we may bear thy corrections with genuine submission of faith, and not continue untameable and obstinate to the last, but return to thee the only fountain of life and salvation, that as thou has once begun in us a good work, so thou mayest perfect it to the day of our Lord. Amen.

Hosea 1:3-7

Grant, Almighty God, that as we were from our beginning lost, when thou wert pleased to extend to us thy hand, and to restore us to salvation for the sake of thy Son; and that as we continue even daily to run headlong to our own ruin, - O grant that we may not, by sinning so often, so provoke at length thy displeasure as to cause thee to take away from us the mercy which thou hast hitherto exercised towards us, and through which thou hast adopted us: but by thy Spirit destroy the wickedness of our heart, and restore us to a sound mind, that we may ever cleave to thee with a true and sincere heart, that being fortified by thy defense, we may continue safe even amidst all kinds of danger, until at length thou gatherest us into that blessed rest, which has been prepared for us in heaven by our Lord Jesus Christ. Amen.

Hosea 1:8-11

Grant, Almighty God, that as we have not only been redeemed from Babylonian exile, but have also emerged from hell itself; for when we were the children of wrath thou didst freely adopt us, and when we were aliens, thou didst in thine infinite goodness open to us the gate of thy kingdom, that we might be made thy heirs through the Son, O grant that we may walk circumspectly before thee, and submit ourselves wholly to thee and to thy Christ, and not feign to be his members, but really prove ourselves to be his body, and to be so governed by his Spirit, that thou mayest at last gather us together into thy celestial kingdom, to which thou daily invitest us by the same Christ our Lord. Amen.

Hosea 2:1-5

Grant, Almighty God, that as thou hast not only of late adopted us as thy children, but before we were born, and as thou hast been pleased to sign us, as soon as we came forth from our mother's womb, with the symbol of that holy redemption, which has been obtained for us by the blood of thy only begotten Son, though we have by our ingratitude renounced so great a benefit, - O grant, that being mindful of our defection and unfaithfulness, of which eve are all guilty, and for which thou hast justly rejected us, we may now with true humility and obedience of faith embrace the grace of thy gospel now again offered to us, by which thou reconciles thyself to us; and grant that we may steadfastly persevere in pure faith, so as never to turn aside from the true obedience of faith, but to advance more and more in the knowledge of thy mercy, that having strong and deep roots, and being firmly grounded in the confidence of sure faith, we may never fall away from the true worship of thee, until thou at length receives us in to that eternal kingdom, which has been procured for us by the blood of thy only Son. Amen.

Hosea 2:6-12

Grant, Almighty God, that inasmuch as we are so dull and slothful, that though often admonished, we yet consider not our sins, yea, though chastised by thy hand, we yet return not immediately to a right mind, - O grant, that we may hereafter profit more under thy rod, and not he refractory and untractable; but as soon as thou raises thy hand, may each of us mourn, know our own evils, and then, with one consent, surrender ourselves to be ruled by thee; and may we, in the meantime, patiently and calmly endure thy chastisements, and never murmur against thee, but ever aspire to the attainment of true repentance, until, having at length put off all the vices and corruptions of our flesh, we attain to the fulness of righteousness, and to that true and blessed glory which has been prepared for us in heaven by Jesus Christ. Amen.

Hosea 2:13-17

Grant, Almighty God, that as we set up against thee so many obstacles through the depravity of our flesh and natural disposition, that we seem as it were to be designedly striving to close up the door against thy goodness and paternal favour, O grant, that our hearts may be so softened by thy Spirit, and the hardness which has hitherto prevailed may be so corrected, that we may submit ourselves to thee with genuine docility, especially as thou dost so kindly and tenderly invite us to thyself, that being allured by thy sweet invitation, we may run, and so run as not to be weary in our course, until Christ shall at length bring us together to thee, and, at the same time, lead us to thee for that eternal life, which he has obtained for us by his own blood. Amen.

Hosea 2:18-23

Grant, Almighty God, that as we are in this life subject to so many miseries, and in the meantime grow insensible in our sins, - O grant that we may learn to search ourselves and consider one sins, that we may be really humbled before thee, and ascribe to ourselves the blame of all our evils, that we may be thus led to a genuine feeling of repentance, and so strive to be reconciled to thee in Christ, that we may wholly depend on thy paternal love, and thus ever aspire to the fulness of eternal felicity, through thy goodness and that immeasurable kindness which thou testifies is ready and offered to all those, who with a sincere heart worship thee, call upon thee, and flee to thee, through Christ our Lord. Amen.

Hosea 3:1-5

Grant, Almighty God, that as thou often dost justly hide thy face from us, so that on every side we see nothing but evidences of thy dreadful judgment, - O grant, that we, with minds raised above the scene of this world, may at the same time cherish the hope which thou constantly settest before us, so that we may feel fully persuaded that we are loved by thee, however severely thou mayest chastise us and may this consolation so support and sustain our souls, that patiently enduring whatever chastisements thou mayest lay upon us, we may ever hold fast the reconciliation which thou hast promised to us in Christ thy Son. Amen.

Hosea 4:1-3

Grant, Almighty God, that since we are at this day as guilty before thee as the Israelites of old were, who were so rebellious against thy Prophets, and that as thou hast often tried sweetly to allure us to thyself without any success, and as we have not hitherto ceased, by our continual obstinacy, to provoke thy wrath, - O grant, that being moved at least by the warnings thou givest us, we may prostrate ourselves before thy face, and not wait until thou puttest forth thy hand to destroy us, but, on the contrary, strive to anticipate thy judgment; and that being at the same time surely convinced that thou art ready to be reconciled to us in Christ, we may flee to Him as our Mediator; and that relying on his intercession, we may not doubt but that thou art ready to give us pardon, until having at length put away all sins, we come to that blessed state of glory which has been obtained for us by the blood of thy Son. Amen.

Hosea 4:4-10

Grant, Almighty God, that, since thou hast hitherto so kindly invited us to thyself, and daily invites us, and often interposes also thy threatening to rouse our inattention, and since we have been inattentive to thy reproofs, as well as to thy paternal kindness, - O grant, that we may not, to the last, proceed in this our wickedness, and thus provoke the vengeance thou here denounces on men past recovery; but that we may anticipate thy wrath by true repentance, and be humbled under thy hand, yea, be thy word, that thou mayest receive us into favor, and nourish us in thy paternal bosom, through Christ our Lord. Amen.

Hosea 4:11-14

Grant, Almighty God, that inasmuch as we are so disposed and inclined to all kinds of errors, to so many and so various forms of superstitions, and as Satan also ceases not to lay in wait for us, and spreads before us his many snares, - O grant, that we may be so preserved in obedience to thee by the teaching of thy word, that we may never turn here and there, either to the right hand or to the left, but continue in that pure worship, which thou hast prescribed, so that we may plainly testify that thou art indeed our Father by continuing under the protection of thy only-begotten Son, whom thou hast given to be our pastor and ruler to the end. Amen.

Hosea 4:15-18

Grant, Almighty God, that since thou hast at this time deigned in thy mercy to gather us to thy Church, and to enclose us within the boundaries of thy word, by which thou preserves us in the true and right worship of thy majesty, - O grant, that we may continue contented in this obedience to thee: and though Satan may, in many ways, attempt to draw us here and there, and we be also ourselves, by nature, inclined to evil, O grant, that being confirmed in faith, and united to thee by that sacred bond, we may yet constantly abide under the guidance of thy word, and thus cleave to Christ thy only-begotten Son, who has joined us for ever to himself, that we may never by any means turn aside from thee, but be, on the contrary, confirmed in the faith of his gospel, until at length he will receive us all into his kingdom. Amen.

Hosea 4:19 – 5:4

Grant, Almighty God, that since thou continues daily to exhort us, and though thou sees us often turning aside from the right course, thou yet ceases not to stretch forth thy hand to us, and also to rouse us by reproofs, that we may repent, - O grant, that we may not be permitted to reject thy word with such perverseness as thou condemnest here in thine ancient people by the mouth of thy Prophet; but rule us by thy Spirit, that we may meekly and obediently submit to thee, and with such teachableness, that if we have not hitherto been willing to become wise, we may not at least be incurable, but suffer thee to heal our diseases, so that we may truly repent, and be so wholly given to obey thee, as never to attempt any thing beyond the rule of thy word, and without that wisdom which thou hast revealed to us, not only by Moses and thy Prophets, but also by thy only-begotten Son, our Lord Jesus Christ. Amen.

Hosea 5:5-9

Grant, Almighty God, that as we are already by nature the children of wrath, and yet thou hast deigned to receive us into favour, and hast set before us a sacred pledge of thy favor in thine only-begotten Son, and that as we have not yet ceased often to provoke thy wrath against us, and also to fall away by shameful perfidy from the covenant thou hast made with us, - O grant, that being at least touched by thy admonitions, we may not harden our hearts in wickedness, but be pliant and teachable, and thus endeavor to return unto favor with thee, that through the interceding sacrifice of thy Son, we may find thee a propitious Father, and be for the future so wholly devoted to thee, that those who shall follow and survive us may be confirmed in the worship of thy majesty, and in true religion, through the same Jesus Christ our Lord. Amen.

Hosea 5:10-15

Grant, Almighty God, that as we continue to kindle often thy wrath against us by our innumerable sins, - O grant, that when thou warnest and wouldest restore us to the right way, we may at least be pliant, and without delay attend to the scourges of thy hand, and not wait for extreme severity, but timely repent; and that we may truly and from the heart seek thee, let us not put on false repentance, but strive to devote ourselves wholly to thee, through Jesus Christ our Lord. Amen.

Hosea 6:1-4

Grant, Almighty God, that as we do not, by due gratitude, respond to thy favors, and after having tasted of thy mercy, have willingly sought ruin to ourselves, - O grant, that we, being renewed by thy

Spirit, may not only remain constant in the fear of thy name, but also advance more and more and be established; that being thus armed with thy invincible power, we may strenuously fight against all the wiles and assaults of Satan, and thus pursue our warfare to the end, - and that being thus sustained by thy mercy, we may ever aspire to that life which is hid for us in heaven, through Jesus Christ our Lord. Amen.

Hosea 6:5-11

Grant, Almighty God, that as we are prone to every kind of wickedness, and are so easily led away to imitate it, when there is any excuse for going astray and any opportunity is offered, - O grant, that being strengthened by the help of thy Spirit, we may continue in purity of faith, and that what we have learnt concerning thee, that thou art a Spirit, may so profit us, that we may worship thee in spirit and with a sincere heart, and never turn aside after the corruptions of the world, nor think that we can deceive thee; but may we so devote our souls and bodies to thee, that our life may in every part of it testify, that we are a pure and holy sacrifice to thee in Christ Jesus our Lord. Amen.

Hosea 7:1-6

Grant, Almighty God, that since thou hast once shone upon us by thy gospel, - O grant, that we may always be guided by this light, and so guided, that all our lusts may be restrained; and may the power of thy Spirit extinguish in us every sinful fervor, that we may not grow hot with our own perverse desires, but that all these being subdued, we may gather new fervor daily, that we may breathe after thee more and more: nor let the coldness of our flesh ever take possession of us, but may we continually advance in the way of piety, until at length we come to that blessed rest, to which thou invites us, and which has been obtained for us by the blood of thy only-begotten Son, our Lord

Jesus Christ. Amen.

Hosea 7:7-12

Grant, Almighty God, that since thou sees us to be so prone to all the allurements of Satan and the world, and at the same time so void of judgment, and carried away by mere levity, - O grant, that by thy Spirit leading us, we may proceed in the right course, on which we have already entered under thy guidance and directing hand, so that we may never go astray from thy word, nor by any means turn aside from pursuing towards the mark which thou hast set before us; and though Satan may attempt to draw us aside, may we yet continue steadfast in thy service, and thus proceed, until we arrive at that blessed rest which, after the warfare of the present life, thou hast promised to us in Christ Jesus our Lord. Amen.

Hosea 7:13 – 8:1

Grant, Almighty God, that since thou continues daily to restore us to thyself, both by scourges and by thy word, though we cease not to go astray after sinful desires, - O grant, that by the direction of thy Spirit, we may at length so return to thee, that we may never afterwards fall away, but be preserved in pure and true obedience, and thus constantly continue in the pure worship of thy majesty and in true, obedience, that after this life past, we may at last reach that blessed rest, which is reserved for us in heaven, through Jesus Christ our Lord. Amen.

Hosea 8:2-7

Grant, Almighty God, that since the rule of thy true and lawful worship is sufficiently known to us, and thou continues to exhort us to persevere in our course, and to abide in that pure and simple worship which thou hast fully approved, - O grant, that we may, in true obedience of faith, respond to thee: and though we now see the whole world carried here and there, and all places full of the awful examples of apostacy, and so much madness everywhere prevailing, that men become more and more hardened daily, - O grant, that, being fortified by invincible faith against these so many temptations, we may persevere in true religion, and never at any time turn aside from the teaching of thy word, until we be at length gathered to Christ our King, under whom, as our head, thou hast promised that we shall ever be safe, and until we attain that happy life which is laid up for us in heaven, through the same Christ our Lord. Amen.

Hosea 8:8-14

Grant, Almighty God, that as we have already so often provoked thy wrath against us, and thou hast in thy paternal indulgence borne with us, or at least chastised us so gently as to spare us, - O grant, that we may not become hardened in our wickedness, but seasonably repent, and that we may not be drawn away after the inventions of our flesh, nor seek ways to flee away from thee, but come straight forward to thy presence, and make a humble, sincere, and honest confession of our sins, that thou mayest receive us into favor, and that being reconciled to us, thou mayest bestow on us a larger measure of thy blessings, through Christ our Lord. Amen.

Hosea 9:1-5

Grant, Almighty God, that inasmuch as thou drawest us at this time to thyself by so many chastisements, While we are yet insensible, through the slothfulness and the indolence of our flesh, - O grant, that Satan may not thus perpetually harden and fascinate us; but that we, being at length awakened, may feel our evils, and be not merely affected by outward punishments, but rouse ourselves, and feel how grievously we have in various ways offended thee, so that we may return to thee with real sorrow, and so abhor ourselves, that we may seek in thee every delight, until we at length offer to thee a pleasing and acceptable sacrifice, by dedicating ourselves and all we have to thee, in sincerity and truth, through Jesus Christ our Lord. Amen.

Hosea 9:6-9

Grant, Almighty God, that as thou shinest on us by thy word, we may not be blind at mid-day, nor wilfully seek darkness, and thus lull our minds asleep: but that exercising ourselves in thy word, we may stir up ourselves more and more to fear thy name, and thus present ourselves, and all our pursuits, as a sacrifice to thee, that thou mayest peaceably rule, and perpetually dwell in us, until thou gatherest us to thy celestial habitation, where there is reserved for us eternal rest and glory, through Jesus Christ our Lord. Amen.

Hosea 9:10-15

Grant, Almighty God, that as thou shinest on us by thy word, we may not be blind at mid-day, nor wilfully seek darkness, and thus lull our minds asleep: but that exercising ourselves in thy word, we may stir up ourselves more and more to fear thy name, and thus present ourselves, and all our pursuits, as a sacrifice to thee, that thou mayest peaceably rule, and perpetually dwell in us, until thou gatherest us to thy celestial habitation, where there is reserved for us eternal rest and glory, through Jesus Christ our Lord. Amen.

Hosea 9:16 – 10:4

Grant, Almighty God, that as thou dost train us up with so much diligence and assiduous care, and regard us as dear and precious like an hereditary vine, - O grant, that we may not bring forth wild grapes, and that our fruit may not be bitter and unpleasant to thee, but that we may strive so to form our whole life in obedience to thy law, that all our actions and thoughts may be pleasant and sweet fruits to thee. And as there is ever some sin mixed up with our works, even when we desire to serve thee sincerely and from the heart, grant that all stains in our works may be so cleansed and washed away by the sacrifice of thy Son, that they may be to thee sacrifices of sweet odour, through the same, even Christ Jesus, who has so reconciled us to thee, as to obtain pardon even for our works. Amen.

Hosea 10:5-9

Grant, Almighty God, that as thou hast once appeared in the person of thy only-begotten Son, and hast rendered in him thy glory visible to us, and as thou dost daily set forth to us the same Christ in the glass of thy gospel, - O grant, that we, fixing our eyes on him, may not go astray, nor be led here and there after wicked inventions, the fallacies of Satan, and the allurements of this world: but may we continue firm in the obedience of faith and persevere in it through the whole course of our life, until we be at length fully transformed into the image of thy eternal glory, which now in part shines in us, through the same Christ our Lord. Amen.

Hosea 10:10-15

Grant, Almighty God, that as we remain yet in our own wickedness, though often warned and sweetly invited by thee, and as thou prevailest not with us by thy daily instruction, - O grant, that we may, in a spirit of meekness, at length turn to thy service, and fight against the hardness and obstinacy of our flesh, till we render ourselves submissive to thee, and not wait until thou puttest forth thy hand against us, or at least so profit under thy chastisements, as not to constrain thee to execute extreme vengeance against us, but to repent without delay; and that we may indeed, without hypocrisy, plough under thy yoke, and so enjoy thy special blessings, that thou mayest show thyself to us not only as our Lord, but also as our Father, full of mercy and kindness, through Christ our Lord. Amen.

Hosea 11:1-5

Grant, Almighty God, that as thou hast deigned to choose us before the foundations of the world were laid, and included us in thy free adoption when we were the children of wrath and doomed to utter ruin, and afterwards embraced us even from the womb, and hast at length favoured us with a clearer proof of thy love, in calling us by thy gospel into a union and communion with thy only-begotten Son, - O grant, that we may not be unmindful of so many and so singular benefits, but respond to thy holy calling, and labour to devote ourselves wholly to thee, and labour, not for one day, but for the whole time designed for us here, both to live and to die according to thy good pleasure, so that we may glorify thee to the end, through our Lord Jesus Christ. Amen.

Hosea 11:6-11

Grant, Almighty God, that since we are too secure and torpid in our sins, thy dread majesty may come to our minds, to humble us, and to remove our fear, that we may learn anxiously to seek reconciliation through Christ, and so abhor ourselves for our sins, that thou mayest then be prepared to receive us: and that unbelief may not shut the door against us, enable us to regard thee to be such as thou hast revealed thyself, and to acknowledge that thou art not like us, but the fountain of all mercy, that we may thus be led to entertain a firm hope of salvation, and that, relying on the Mediator, thy only-begotten Son, we may know him as the throne of grace, full of compassion and mercy. O grant, that we may thus come to thee, that through him we may certainly know that thou art our Father, so that the covenant thou hast made with us may never fail through our fault, even this, that we are thy people, because thou hast once adopted us in thy only-begotten Son, our Lord Jesus Christ. Amen.

Hosea 11:12 – 12:5

Grant, Almighty God, that inasmuch as thou showest thyself to us at this day so kindly as a Father, having presented to us a singular and an invaluable pledge of thy favour in thy only begotten Son, - O grant, that we may entirely devote ourselves to thee, and truly render thee that free service and obedience which is due to a Father, so that we may have no other object in life but to confirm that adoption, with which thou hast once favoured us, until we at length, being gathered into thy eternal kingdom, shall partake of its fruit, together with Christ Jesus thy Son. Amen.

Hosea 12:6-7

Grant, Almighty God, that as thou appearest not now to us in shadows and types, as formerly to the holy fathers, but clearly and plainly in thy only-begotten Son, - O grant, that we may be wholly given to the contemplation of thine image, which thus shines before us; and that we may in such a manner be transformed into it, as to make increasing advances, until at length, having put off all the filth of our flesh, we be fully conformed to that pure and perfect holiness which dwells in Christ, as in him dwells the fulness of all blessings and thus obtain at last a participation of that glory which our Lord has procured for us by his resurrection. Amen.

Hosea 12:8-14

Grant, Almighty God, that as we have not only been created by thee, but when thou hast placed us in this world, thou hast also enriched us with abundance of all blessings, - O grant, that we may not transfer to others the glory duo to thee, and that especially since we are daily admonished by thy word, and even severely reproved, we may not with an iron hardness resist, but render ourselves pliable to thee, and not give ourselves up to our own devices, but follow with true docility and meekness, that rule which thou hast prescribed in thy word, until at length having put off all the remains of errors, we shall enjoy that blessed light, which thou hast prepared for us in heaven, through Jesus Christ our Lord. Amen.

Hosea 13:1-6

Grant, Almighty God, that as thou dost so kindly call on us daily by thy voice, meekly and calmly to offer ourselves to be ruled by thee, and since thou hast exalted us to a high degree of honour by freeing us from the dread of the devil, and from that tyranny which kept us in miserable fear, and hast also favoured us with the Spirit of adoption and of hope, - O grant, that we, being mindful of these benefits, may ever submit ourselves to thee, and desire only to raise our voice for this end, that the whole world may submit itself to thee, and that those who seem now to rage against thee may at length be brought, as well as we, to render thee obedience, so that thy Son Christ may be the Lord of all, to the end that thou alone mayest be exalted, and that we may be made subject to thee, and be at length raised up above, and become partakers of that glory which has been obtained for us by Christ our Lord. Amen.

Hosea 13:7-13

Grant, Almighty God, that as thou hast given us thy only begotten Son to rule us, and hast by thy good pleasure consecrated him a King over us, that we may be perpetually safe and secure under his hand against all the attempts of the devil and of the whole world, - O grant, that we may suffer ourselves to be ruled by his authority, and so conduct ourselves, that he may ever continue to watch for our safety: and as thou hast committed us to him, that he may be the guardian of our salvation, so also suffer us not either to turn aside or to fall, but preserve us ever in his service, until we be at length gathered into that blessed and everlasting kingdom, which has been procured for us by the blood of thy only Son. Amen.

Hosea 13:14 – 14:2

Grant, Almighty God, that as we now carry about us this mortal body, yea, and nourish through sin a thousand deaths within us, - O grant, that we may ever by faith direct our eyes towards heaven, and to that incomprehensible power, which is to be manifested at the last day by Jesus Christ our Lord, so that in the midst of death we may hope that thou wilt be our Redeemer, and enjoy that redemption, which he completed when he rose from the dead; and not doubt but that the fruit which he then brought forth by his Spirit will come also to us, when Christ himself shall come to judge the world; and may we thus walk in the fear of thy name, that we may be really gathered among his members, to be made partakers of that glory, which by his death he has procured for us. Amen.

Hosea 14:3-7

Grant, Almighty God, that as we are so miserable as soon as thou withdrawest thy favour from us, - O grant, that we may deeply feel this conviction, and thus learn to be humble before thee, and to hate our ownselves, and that we may not in the mean lime deceive ourselves by such allurements as commonly prevail, to put our hope in creatures or in this world, but raise our minds upwards to thee, and fix on thee our hearts, and never doubt, but that when thou embraces us with thy paternal love, nothing shall be wanting to us. And in the meantime, may we suppliantly flee to thy mercy, and with true and genuine confession, acknowledge this to be our only protection - that thou deign to receive us into favour, and to abolish our sins, into which we not only daily fall, but by which we also deserve eternal death, so that we may daily rise through thy free pardon, till at length our Redeemer Christ thy Son shall appear to us from heaven. Amen.

JOEL

Joel 1:1-4

Grant, Almighty God that as almost the whole world give such loose reins to their licentiousness, that they hesitate not either to despise or to regard as of no value thy sacred word - Grant, O Lord that we may always retain such reverence as is justly due to it and to thy holy oracles and be so moved whenever thou deignest to address us that being truly humbled, we may be raised up by faith to heaven, and by hope gradually attain that glory which is as yet hid from us. And may we at the same time so submissively restrain ourselves, as to make it our whole wisdom to obey thee and to do thee service, until thou gatherest us into thy kingdom, where we shall be partakers of thy glory, through Christ our Lord. Amen.

Joel 1:5-11

Grant, Almighty God, that as thou invites us daily by various means to repentance, and continues also to urge us, because thou sees our extreme tardiness, - O grant that we may at length be awakened from our indifference, and suffer us not to be inebriated by the charms of Satan and the world; but by thy Spirit rouse us to real groaning, that, being ashamed of ourselves, we may flee to thy mercy, and doubt not but that thou wilt be propitious to us, provided with a sincere heart we call on thee, and seek that reconciliation which thou daily offerest to us by thy Gospel in the name of thy only begotten Son. Amen.

Joel 1:12-20

Grant, Almighty God, that as thou sees us to be surrounded with the infirmity of our flesh, and so held by, and, as it were, overwhelmed with, earthly cares, that we can hardly raise up our hearts and minds to thee, - O grant, that being awaked by thy word and daily warnings, we may at length feel our evils, and that we may not only learn by the stripes thou inflictest on us, but also of our own accord, summon ourselves to judgment, and examine our hearts, and thus come to thy presence, being our own judges; so that we may anticipate thy displeasure, and thus obtain that mercy which thou best promised to all, who, turning only to thee, deprecate thy wrath, and also hope for thy favor, through the name of one Lord Jesus Christ. Amen.

Joel 2:1-11

Grant, almighty God, that as thou invites us daily with so much kindness and love, and makes known to us thy paternal goodwill, which thou didst once show to us in Christ thy Son, - O grant, that, being allured by thy goodness, we may surrender ourselves wholly to thee, and become so teachable and submissive, that wherever thou guidest us by thy Spirit thou mayest follow us with every blessing: let us not, in the meantime, be deaf to thy warnings; and whenever we deviate from the right way, grant that we may immediately awake when thou warnest us, and return to the right path, and deign thou also to embrace us and reconcile us to thyself through Christ our Lord. Amen.

Joel 2:12-14

Grant, Almighty God, that as thou seest us so foolish in nourishing our vices, and also so ensnared by the gratifications of the flesh, that without being constrained we hardly return to thee, - O grant, that we may feel the weight of thy wrath, and be so touched with the dread of it, as to return gladly to thee, laying aside every dissimulation, and devote ourselves so entirely to thy service, that it may appear that we have from the heart repented, and that We have not trifled with thee by an empty pretense, but have offered to thee our hearts as a sacrifice, so that we and all our works might be sacred offerings to thee through our whole life, that thy name may be glorified in us through Christ our Lord. Amen.

Joel 2:15-20

Grant, Almighty God, that as we continue to excite thy wrath against us, and are so insensible, though thou exhortest us daily to repentance, - O grant, that what thy Prophet teaches may penetrate into our hearts, and be like a sounding trumpet, that we may be really and sincerely made humble before thee, and be so touched with the sense of thy wrath, that we may learn to put off all the depraved affections of our flesh, and not merely to deplore the sins we have already committed: and do thou also look upon us in future, that we may diligently walk in thy fear, and consecrate ourselves wholly to thee; and as thou hast deigned to choose us for thine inheritance, and gather us under thy Christ, may we so live under him as our leader, until we be at length gathered into thy celestial kingdom to enjoy that happy rest, which thou hast promised to us, and which thou promisest also daily, and which has been purchased by the blood of the same, our Lord Jesus Christ. Amen.

Joel 2:21-28

Grant, Almighty God, that since we want so many aids while in this frail life, and as it is a shadowy life, we cannot pass a moment, except thou dost continually, and at all times, supply through thy bounty what is needful, - O grant, that we may so profit by thy so many benefits, that we may learn to raise our minds upwards, and ever aspire after celestial life, to which by thy gospel thou invites us so kindly and sweetly every day, that being gathered into thy celestial kingdom, we may enjoy that perfect felicity, which has been procured for us by the blood of thy Son, our Lord Jesus Christ. Amen.

Joel 2:29-31

Grant, Almighty God, that as we are now surrounded on every side by so many miseries, and as our condition is such, that amidst groans and continual sorrows, our life could be hardly sustained without being supported by spiritual grace, - O grant, that we may learn to look on the face of thine Anointed, and seek comfort from him, and such a comfort as may not engross our minds, or at least not retain us in the world, but raise our thoughts to heaven, and daily sell to our hearts the testimony of our adoption, and that though many evils must be borne by us in this world, we may yet continue to pursue our course, and to fight and to strive with invincible perseverance, until having at length finished all our struggles, we reach that blessed rest, which has been obtained for us by the blood of thy only-begotten Son, our Lord Jesus Christ. Amen.

Joel 2:32 – 3:3

Grant, Almighty God, that as thou not only invites us continually by the voice of thy Gospel to seek thee, but also offerest to us thy Son as our Mediator, through whom an access to thee is open, that we may find thee a propitious Father, - O grant, that relying on thy kind invitation, we may through life exercise ourselves in prayer: and as so many evils disturb us on all sides, and so many wants distress and oppress us, may we be led more earnestly to call on thee, and, in the meantime, be never wearied in this exercise of prayer; that, being through life heard by thee, we may at length be gathered to thy eternal kingdom, where we shall enjoy that salvation which thou hast promised to us, and of which also thou daily testifiest to us by thy Gospel, and be for ever united to thy only begotten Son, of whom we are how members; that we may be partakers of all the blessings, which he has obtained for us by his death. Amen.

Joel 3:4-11

Grant, Almighty God, that as we are assailed on every side by enemies, and as not only the wicked according to the flesh are incensed against us, but Satan also musters his forces and contrives in various ways to ruin us, - O grant, that we being furnished with the courage thy Spirit bestows, may fight to the end under thy guidance and never be wearied under any evils. And may we, at the same time, be humbled under thy mighty hand when it pleases thee to afflict us and so sustain all our troubles that with a courageous mind we may strive for that victory which thou promises to us, and that having completed all our struggles we may at length attain that blessed rest which is reserved for us in heaven through Jesus Christ our Lord. Amen.

Joel 3:12-21

Grant, Almighty God, that as we have, in this world, to fight continually, not only with one kind of enemies, but with numberless enemies, and not only with flesh and blood, but also with the devil, the prince of darkness, - O grant, that, being armed with thy power, we may persevere in this contest; and when thou afflictest us for our sins, may we learn to humble ourselves, and so submit to thy authority, that we may hope for the redemption promised to us; and though tokens of thy displeasure may often appear to us, may we yet ever raise up our minds by hope to heaven, and from thence look for thy only begotten Son, until, coming as the Judge of the world, he gathers us and brings us to the fruition of that blessed and eternal life, which he has obtained for us by his own blood. Amen.

AMOS

Amos 1:1-5

Grant, Almighty God, that as thou seest us to be of a disposition so hard and rebellious, that we are not, without great difficulty, drawn to thee, - O grant, that we may at least be subdued by the threatenings thou daily denouncest on us, and be so subdued, that being also drawn by thy word, we may give up ourselves to thee, and not only suffer ourselves to be constrained by punishments and collections, but also obey thee with a willing mind, and most readily offer ourselves to thee as a sacrifice of obedience, so that being ruled by the Spirit of thy Son, we may at length attain that blessed rest, which has been prepared for us by the same thy Son our Lord. Amen.

Amos 1:6-15

Grant, Almighty God, that since thou hast designed, by so many examples, to teach the world the fear of thy name, we may improve under thy mighty hand, and not abuse thy forbearance, nor gather for ourselves a treasure of dreadful vengeance by our obstinacy and irreclaimable wickedness, but seasonably repent while thou invites us, and while it is the accepted time, and while thou offerest to us reconciliation, that being brought to nothing in ourselves, we may gather courage through grace, which is offered to us through Christ our Lord. Amen.

Amos 2:1-7

Grant, almighty God, that since we see so grievous punishments formerly executed on unbelievers who had never tasted of the pure knowledge of thy word, we may be warned by their example, so as to abstain from all wickedness, and to continue in pure obedience to thy word; and that, as thou hast made known to us that thou hatest all those superstitions and depravations by which we turn aside from thy word, - O grant, that we may ever be attentive to that role which has been prescribed to us by thee in the Law, as well as in the Prophets and in the Gospel, so that we may constantly abide in thy precepts, and be wholly dependent on the words of thy month, and never turn aside either to the right hand or to the left, but glorify thy name, as thou has commanded us, by offering to thee a true, sincere, and spiritual worship, through Christ our Lord. Amen.

Amos 2:8-13

Grant, Almighty God, that as thou hast not only redeemed us by the blood of thy only begotten Son, but also guides us during our earthly pilgrimage, and suppliest us with whatever is needful, - O grant, that we may not be unmindful of so many favors, and turn away from thee and follow our sinful desires, but that we may continue bound to thy service, and never burden thee with our sins, but submit ourselves willingly to thee in true obedience, that by glorifying thy name we may carry thee both in body and soul, until thou at length gatherest us into that blessed kingdom which has been obtained for us by the blood of thy Son. Amen.

Amos 2:14 – 3:8

Grant, Almighty God, that as thou art pleased daily to exhort us to repentance, and dost not suddenly execute thy judgment by which we might be in an instant overwhelmed, but givest us time to seek reconciliation, - O grant, that we may now attend to thy teaching, and all thy admonitions and threatenings, and become teachable and obedient to thee, lest thou be constrained on finding us hardened against thy threatening, and wholly irreclaimable, to bring on us extreme vengeance: make us then so to submit ourselves to thee in the spirit of teachableness and obedience, that being placed under the protection of thy Son, we may truly call on thee as our Father, and find thee to be so in reality, when thou shalt show to us that paternal love, which thou hast promised, and which we have all experienced from the beginning, who have truly and from the heart called on thy name, through the same, even Christ our Lord. Amen.

Amos 3:9-14

Grant, Almighty God, that inasmuch as we so provoke thee daily by our sins, that we are worthy of eternal destruction, and no good remains in us, and though we are severely chastised with temporal punishments, thou dost not yet take from us the hope of that mercy, which thou hast promised in thy Son to those who truly and from the heart repent and call on thee as their Father, - O grant, that being touched with the sense of our evils, we may, in true humility, and with the genuine feeling of penitence, offer ourselves as a sacrifice to thee, and seek pardon with such groaning, that having undergone temporal punishments, we may finally enjoy that grace which is laid up for all sinners, who truly and from the heart turn to thee and implore that mercy which has been prepared for all those who really prove themselves to be the members of thine only begotten Son. Amen.

Amos 3:15 – 4:6

Grant, Almighty God, that as thou wouldest have our life to be formed by the rule of thy law, and hast revealed in it what pleaseth thee, that we may not wander in uncertainty but render thee obedience, - O grant, that we may wholly submit ourselves to thee, and not only devote our life and all our labors to thee, but also offer to thee as a sacrifice our understanding and whatever prudence and reason we may possess, so that by spiritually serving thee, we may really glorify thy name, through Christ our Lord. Amen

Amos 4:7-13

Grant, Almighty God, that since by thy word thou kindly invites us to thyself, we may not turn deaf ears to thee, but anticipate thy rod and scourges; and that when, for the stupidity and thoughtlessness by which we have become inebriated, thou addest those punishments by which thou sharply urgest us to repent, - O grant, that we may not continue wholly intractable, but at length turn our hearts to thy service and submit ourselves to the yoke of thy word, and that we may be so instructed by the punishments, which thou hast inflicted on us and still inflictest, that we may truly and from the heart turn to thee, and offer ourselves to thee as a sacrifice, that thou mayest govern us according to thy will, and so rule all our affections by thy Spirit, that we may through the whole of our life strive to glorify thy name in Christ Jesus, thy Son our Lord. Amen.

Amos 5:1-7

Grant, Almighty God, that as thou seest us to be so entangled, not only by depraved lusts, but also by the allurements of Satan, and by our own ignorance and blindness, - O grant, that being roused by thy word we may at the same time learn to open our eyes to thy wholesome warnings by which thou callest us to thyself: and since we cannot do this without thy Spirit being our guide and leader, grant that he may enlighten our eyes, to the end that, being truly and from the heart tarried to thee, we may know that thou art propitious and ready to hear all who unfeignedly seek thee, and that, being reconciled to thee in Christ, we may also know that thou art to us a propitious Father, and that thou wilt bestow on us all kinds of blessings, until thou at length gatherest us to thy celestial kingdom, through Christ our Lord. Amen.

Amos 5:8-13

Grant, Almighty God, that as we cannot see with our eyes thy infinite and incomprehensible glory, which is hid from us, we may learn at least by thy works, what thy great power is, so as to be humbled under thy mighty hand, and never trifle with thee as hypocrites are wont to do; but to bring a heart really sincere, and also pure hands, that our whole life may testify that a true fear of thy name prevails, in our hearts: and grant, that whilst we devote ourselves wholly to thy service, we may courageously and with invincible hearts, fight against all these corruptions, by which we are on every side beset, until, having finished our warfare, we attain to that celestial rest, which has been prepared for us by Jesus Christ our Lord. Amen.

Amos 5:14-20

Grant, Almighty God, that seeing we are so sleepy, yea, so fascinated by our sins, that nothing is more difficult than to put off our own nature and to renounce that wickedness to which we have become habituated, - O grant, that we, being really awakened by thy scourgings, may truly return to thee, and that, having wholly changed our disposition and renounced all wickedness, we may sincerely, and from the heart, submit ourselves to thee, and so look forward to the coming of thy Son, that we may cheerfully and joyfully wait for him, by ever striving after such a renovations of life as may strip us of our flesh and all corruptions, until, being at length renewed after thine image, we become partakers of that glory, which has been obtained for us by the blood of the same, thy only-begotten Son. Amen.

Amos 5:21-27

Grant, Almighty God, that as thou seest us to be so prone to corrupt superstitions, and that we are with so much difficulty restrained by thy word, - O grant, that we being confirmed by thy Spirit, may never turn aside either to the right hand or to the left, but be ever attentive to thee alone, and not worship thee presumptuously, nor pollute thy worship with our outward pomps, but call on thee with a sincere heart, and, recumbing on thy aid, flee to thee in all our necessities, and never abuse thy holy name, which thou hast designed to be engraven on us, but be conformed to the image of thy Son, that thou mayest be to us truly a Father, and that we may be thy children, in the name of the same Christ our Lord. Amen.

Amos 6:1-7

Grant, Almighty God, that since thou showest thyself at this day to be justly offended with us, and our own consciences reprove us, inasmuch as dreadful tokens appear, by which we may learn how much and in how many ways we have provoked thy wrath, - O grant, that we may be really touched with the consciousness of our evils, and being afflicted in our hearts, may be so humbled, that without any outward affliction, we may wholly submit ourselves to be reproved by thee, and at the same time flee to that mercy which is laid up for us, and which thou daily offerest to us in Christ Jesus our Lord. Amen.

Amos 6:8-14

Grant, Almighty God, that since we are extremely deaf to those so many holy warnings by which thou continuest to recall us to thyself, and since we ever harden ourselves against those threatenings, by which thou terrifiest us, that thou mayest break or at least correct our hardness, - O grant, that we may, though late, yet in time, before final vengeance comes, attend to thy word and submit ourselves to thee, and in a teachable spirit undertake thy yoke, that thou mightest receive us into favor, and vouchsafe to us thy paternal kindness, and being at length reconciled to us, thou might grant us thy blessings, which thou hast promised to all thy children, who are the members of thy only begotten Son our Lord. Amen.

Amos 7:1-9

Almighty God, since thou so suspendest thy hand in chastising us, that except we be wholly blind and stupid, we must acknowledge that we are spared in order that we may willingly return to thee, and that being allured by the gentleness of thy forbearance, we may submit ourselves to thee in willing obedience, - O grant, that we may not harden our hearts, nor be slow, nor slothful, nor even backward to repent, when thou deferrest extreme punishment, but strive to anticipate thy final vengeance, and so submit ourselves to thee, that we may be pardoned while it is time, and so hasten to offer our hearts whole and sincere to thee, and so repent, while urged by extreme danger, that there may not remain any hidden hypocrisy in our hearts, but that we may in such a way search every faculty of our soul, that thou mayest become to us a real and faithful witness of that integrity which thou requires of all who return to thee to obtain pardon through Jesus Christ our Lord. Amen.

Amos 7:10-15

Grant, Almighty God, that inasmuch as thou permittest reins so loose to Satan, that he attempts, in all manner of ways, to subvert thy servants, - O grant, that they who have been sent and moved by thee, and at the same time furnished with the invincible strength of thy Spirit, may go on perseveringly to the last in the discharge of their office: and whether their adversaries assails them by crafts, or oppose them by open violence, may they not desist from their course, but devote themselves wholly to thee, with prudence as well as with courage, that they may thus persevere in continual obedience: and do thou also dissipate all the mists and all the crafts which Satan spreads to deceive the inexperienced, until at length the truth emerge, which is the conqueror of the devil and of the whole world, and until thy Son, the Sun of Righteousness, appear, that he may gather the whole world, that in thy rest we may enjoy the victory, which is to be daily obtained by us in our constant struggles with the enemies of the same, thine only Son. Amen.

Amos 7:16 – 8:5

Grant, Almighty, that as thou ceases not daily to warn us in time to repent and anticipate thy judgment, - O grant, that we may not be so deaf and slow, as to delay until our vices be ripened, lest no remedy should remain for us; but, on the contrary, that being tamed and subdued by thy threatening, we may flee to thy mercy, and so consider thy judgments while at a distance, that we may not provoke thy wrath by our perverseness, but rather dispose thee to pardon by striving to be reconciled to thee in the name of Christ thy Son, and by doing this not only with the mouth and tongue, or by any other outward means, but also with a real feeling of heart and a life corresponding thereto, so that we may present ourselves in uprightness and sincerity, as thy children, that thou mayest also show thyself as a Father to us in the same Christ, thy Son, our Lord. Amen.

Amos 8:6-12

Grant, Almighty God, that as thou continues to recall us to thyself, and though thou sees us to be alienated from thee, thou yet dost extend thy hand to us, and often exhort and stimulate us by holy admonitions, and even frighten us by punishments, that we may not run headlong to our own ruin, - O grant, that we may not be deaf to admonitions so holy and gracious, nor be hardened against thy threatening, but that we may become instantly submissive, and also return to the right way and constantly proceed in it, and follow one vocation through our whole life, as long as thou continues it to us, until we at length reach the mark which is set before us, even until we be gathered into thy celestial kingdom, through Jesus Christ our Lord. Amen.

Amos 8:13 – 9:6

Grant, Almighty God, that as thou hast showed to us by evidences so remarkable that all things are under thy command, and that we, who live in this world through thy favor, are as nothing, for thou couldest reduce us to nothing in a moment, - O grant, that being conscious of thy power, we may reverently fear thy hand, and be wholly devoted to thy glory; and as thou kindly offerest thyself to us as a Father, may we be drawn by this kindness, and surrender ourselves wholly to thee by a willing obedience, and never labor for any thing through life but to glorify thy name, as thou hast redeemed us through thy only begotten Son, that so we may also enjoy through him that eternal inheritance which is laid up for us in heaven. Amen.

Amos 9:7-12

Grant, Almighty God, that as we see everywhere so many evident tokens of thy displeasure, and more grievous ones are impeding, if we indeed duly consider how grievously we have provoked thy wrath, and how wickedly also the whole world at this day rages against thee and at the same time abuses thy many and excellent benefits, - O grant, that we may ever remember thy covenant and entertain a perpetual confidence in thy only-begotten Son, that whenever it may please thee to sift us, thou mayest keep us in safety, until we come, not into any earthly storehouse but into thy celestial kingdom, where we may become partakers of that glory which thy Son has obtained for us, who has once for all redeemed us that we may ever remain under his guardianship and protection. Amen. [There is no prayer for the rest of the chapter – you will need to make up your own !]

OBADIAH

Obadiah 1-4

Grant, Almighty God, that as thou seest us to be on every side at this day beset by so many enemies, even by those who constantly devise means to destroy us, while we are so very weak and feeble, - O grant, that we may learn to look up to thee, and that our trust may so recumb on thee, that however exposed we may be to all kinds of danger according to what appears to the flesh, we may not yet doubt but that thou art ever armed with sufficient power to terrify our enemies, so that we may quietly live even amidst all dangers, and never cease to call on thy name, as thou hast promised to be the sure and faithful defender of our safety in Christ Jesus our Lord. Amen.

Obadiah 5-11

Grant Almighty God, that as thou hast once received us under thy protection, and hast promised that our salvation would be so much cared for by thee, that whatever Satan and the whole world may contrive, thou wilt yet keep us safe and secure, - O grant, that being endued with perseverance, we may remain within our borders, and be not carried away here and there either by craft or by wicked counsels; but be thou pleased to keep us in genuine integrity, that being protected by thy help, we may, by experience, find that true which thou declarest in thy word, that they who call on thee in truth shall ever know thee to be propitious to them: and since thou hast already made open to us an access to thee in the person of thy only - begotten Son, O grant, that we the sheep, may rely on him as our shepherd, and resignedly abide under his protection until we be removed from all dangers into that eternal rest, which has been obtained for us by the blood of thy Son Jesus Christ. Amen.

Obadiah 12-21

Grant, Almighty God, that as we are so scattered in our pilgrimage in this world, that even a dreadful spectacle is presented to our eyes, when we see thy Church so miserably rent asunder, O grant, that being endued with the real power of thy Spirit, and gathered into one, we may so cultivate brotherly kindness among ourselves, that each may strive to help another, and at the same time keep our eyes fixed on Christ Jesus; and though hard contests may await us, may we yet be under his care and protection, and so exercise patience, that having finished our warfare, we may at last enjoy that blessed rest, which thou hast promised to us, and which is laid up for us in heaven, and which has also been purchased for us by the blood of Christ thy Son, one Lord. Amen.

JONAH

Jonah 1:1-3

Grant, Almighty God, that as thou hast not sent a Jonah to us, when alienated from every hope of salvation, but hast given thy Son to be our Teacher, clearly to show to us the way of salvation, and not only to call us to repentance by threatening and terrors, but also kindly to allure us to the hope of eternal life, and to be a pledge of thy paternal love, - O grant, that we may not reject so remarkable a favor offered to us, but willingly and from the heart obey thee; and though the condition which thou settest before us in thy Gospel may seem hard, and though the bearing of the cross is bitter to our flesh, yet may we never shun to obey thee, but present ourselves to thee as a sacrifice; and having overcome all the hindrances of this world, may we thus proceed in the course of our holy calling, until we be at length gathered into thy celestial kingdom, under the guidance of Christ thy Son, our Lord. Amen.

Jonah 1:4-7

Grant, Almighty God, that though we are here disquieted in the midst of so many tossings, we may yet learn with tranquil minds to recumb on thy grace and promise, by which thou testifiest that thou wilt be ever near us, and not wait until by a strong hand thou drawest us to thyself, but that we may be, on the contrary, ever attentive to thy providence: may we know that our life not only depends on a thread, but also vanishes like the smoke, unless thou protectest it, so that we may recumb wholly on thy power; and may we also, while in a cheerful and quiet state, so call on thee, that relying on thy protection we may live in safety, and at the same time be careful, lest torpor, which draws away our minds and thoughts from meditating on the divine life, should creep over us, but may we, on the contrary, so earnestly seek thee, morning and evening, and at all times, that we may through life advance towards the mark thou hast set before us, until we at length reach that heavenly kingdom, which Christ thy Son has obtained for us by his own blood. Amen

Jonah 1:8-12

Grant, Almighty God that as thou urgest us daily to repentance and each of us is also stung with the consciousness of his own sins, - grant, that we may not grow stupid in our vices, nor deceive ourselves with empty flatteries, but that each of us may, on the contrary carefully examine his own life and then with one mouth and heart confess that we are all guilty not only of light offenses, but of such as deserve eternal death, and that no other relief remains for us but thine infinite mercy and that we may so seek to become partakers of that grace which has been once offered to us by thy Son, and is daily offered to us by his Gospel, that, relying on him as our Mediator, we may not cease to entertain hope even in the midst of thousand deaths, until we be gathered into that blessed life, which has been procured for us by the blood of thy only Son. Amen.

Jonah 1:13-17

Grant, Almighty God, that as thou settest before us this day thy holy Prophet as an awful example of thy wrath against all who are rebellious and disobedient to thee, - O grant, that we may learn so to subject all our thoughts and affections to thy word, that we may not reject any thing that pleases thee, but so learn both to live and to die to thee, that we may ever regard thy will, and undertake nothing but what thou hast testified is approved by thee, so that we may fight under thy banners, and through life obey thy word, until at length we reach that blessed rest which has been obtained for us by the blood of thy only begotten Son, and is laid up for us in heaven through the hope of his Gospel. Amen.

Jonah 2:1-7

Grant, Almighty God, that as thou hast once given us such an evidence of thy infinite power in thy servant Jonah, whose mind, when he was almost sunk down into hell, thou hadst yet raised up to thyself, and hadst so supported with firm constancy, that he ceased not to pray and to call on thee, - O grant, that in the trials by which we must be daily exercised, we may raise upwards our minds to thee, and never cease to think that thou art near us; and that when the signs of thy wrath appear, and when our sins thrust themselves before our eyes, to drive us to despair, may we still constantly struggle, and never surrender the hope of thy mercy, until having finished all our contests, we may at length freely and fully give thanks to thee, and praise thy infinite goodness, such as we daily experience that being conducted through continual trials, we may at last come into that blessed rest which is laid up for us in heaven, through Christ one Lord. Amen.

Jonah 1:8 – 3:5

Grant, Almighty God, that as there is so much timidity in us, that none of us is prepared to follow where thou mayest call us, we may be so instructed by the example of thy servant Jonah, as to obey thee in every thing, and that though Satan and the world may oppose us with all their terrors, we may yet be strengthened by a reliance on thy power and protection, which thou hast promised to us, and may go on in the course of our vocation, and never turn aside, but thus contend against all the hindrances of this world, until we reach that celestial kingdom, where we shall enjoy thee and Christ thy only begotten Son, who is our strength and our salvation: and may thy Spirit quicken us, and strengthen all our faculties, that we may obey thee, and that at length thy name may be glorified in us, through Christ our Lord. Amen.

Jonah 3:6-10

Grant, Almighty God, that as we are loaded with so many vices, and so many sins, yea, and scandalous crimes break out daily among us, - O Grant, that we may not be hardened against so many exhortations, by which thou invites us to thyself, but that being made contrite in spirit, whenever thou denounces on us thy wrath, we may be really humbled, and so place ourselves before thy tribunal, that we may, by a true confession and genuine fear, anticipate the judgment which would otherwise have been prepared for us; and that in the meantime relying on Christ our Mediator, we may entertain such a hope of pardon as may raise us up to thee, and not doubt but that thou art ready to embrace us, when we shall be moved by a true and real feeling of fear and penitence, since it is a proof of thy favor, when thou art pleased to anticipate us, and by thy Spirit testifies that thou art a Father to us; and, in a word, may we be so cast down in ourselves, as to raise up our hope even to heaven, through Jesus Christ one Lord. Amen.

Jonah 4:1-4

Grant, Almighty God, that as thou sees us implicated in so many errors, that we often fall through want of thought, and as thou also sees that the violent emotions of our flesh wholly blind whatever reason and judgment there is in us, - O grant, that we may learn to give up ourselves altogether to obey thee, and so honor thy wisdom as never to contend with thee, though all things may happen contrary to our wishes, but patiently to wait for such an issue as it may please thee to grant; and may we never be disturbed by any of the hindrances which Satan may throw in our way, but ever go on towards the mark which thou hast set before us, and never turn aside from thee, until, having gone through all dangers and overcome all impediments, we shall at length reach that blessed rest, which has been obtained for us by the blood of thy Son. Amen.

Jonah 4:5-11

Grant, Almighty God, that as thou hast, in various ways, testified, and daily continues to testify, how dear and precious to thee are mankind, and as we enjoy daily so many and so remarkable proofs of thy goodness and favor, - O grant, that we may learn to rely wholly on thy goodness, many examples of which thou settest before us, and which thou wouldest have us continually to experience, that we may not only pass through our earthly course, but also confidently aspire to the hope of that blessed and celestial life which is laid up for us in heaven, through Christ our Lord. Amen.

MICAH

Micah 1:1-5

Grant, Almighty God, that, since to a perverse, and in every way a rebellious people, thou didst formerly show so much grace, as to exhort them continually to repentance, and to stretch forth thy hand to them by thy Prophets, - O grant, that the same word may sound in our ears; and when we do not immediately profit by thy teaching, O cast us not away, but, by thy Spirit, so subdue all our thoughts and affections, that we, being humbled, may give glory to thy majesty, such as is due to thee, and that, being allured by thy paternal favor, we may submit ourselves to thee, and, at the same time, embrace that mercy which thou offerest and presentest to us in Christ, that we may not doubt but thou wilt be a Father to us, until we shall at length enjoy that eternal inheritance, which has been obtained for us by the, blood of thine only-begotten Son. Amen.

Micah 1:6-14

Grant, Almighty God, that, being warned by so many examples, the record of which thou hast designed to continue to the end of the world, that we may learn how dreadful a judge thou art to the perverse, - O grant, that we may not, at this day, be deaf to thy teaching, which is conveyed to us by the mouth of thy Prophet, but that we may strive to be so reconciled to thee, that, passing by all men, we may present ourselves unreservedly to thee, so that, relying on thy mercy alone which thou hast promised to us in Christ, we may not doubt but thou wilt be propitious to us, and be so touched with the spirit of true penitence, that, if we have been to others a bad example and an offense, we may lead others to the right way of salvation, and each of us may so endeavor to assist our neighbors in a holy life, that we may together attain that blessed and celestial life, which thine only-begotten Son has procured for us by his own blood. Amen.

Micah 1:15 – 2:6

Grant, Almighty God, that as thou art pleased to try our patience by requiring mutual justice and the offices of love and benevolence, - O Grant, that we may not be wolves one to another, but show ourselves to be really thy children, by observing all those duties of justice and kindness which thou commandest, and thus follow what is right and just through the whole course of our life, that we may at length enjoy that blessedness which is laid up for us in heaven, through Christ our Lord. Amen.

Micah 2:7-11

Grant, Almighty God, that since we cannot otherwise really profit by thy word, than by having all our thoughts and affections subjected to thee, and offered to thee as a sacrifice, - O grant, that we may suffer thee, by the sound of thy word, so to pierce through everything within us, that being dead in ourselves, we may live to thee, and never suffer flatteries to become our ruin but that we may, on the contrary, patiently endure reproofs, however bitter they may be, only let them serve to us as medicine, by which our inward vices may be cleansed, until at length being thoroughly cleansed and formed into new creatures, we may, by a pious and holy life, really glorify thy name, and be received into that celestial glory, which has been purchased for us by the blood of thy only-begotten Son, our Lord Jesus Christ. Amen.

Micah 2:12 – 3:5

Grant, Almighty God, that as thou wouldest have the image of thy justice to shine in princes, and whom thou arrest with the sword, that they might rule in thy name, and be really thy ministers, - O grant, that this thy blessing may openly appear among us, and that by this evidence thou mayest testify that thou art not only propitious to us, but hadst also a care for our safety, and watches over our welfare and well-being: and do thou so shine by thy word, that it may never be obscured or clouded among us through any depraved cupidity, but ever retain its own clear purity, so that we may proceed in the right path of salvation, which thou hast discovered and prescribed, until we be at length gathered into thy celestial kingdom, to enjoy that eternal inheritance, which has been procured for us by the blood of thy only-begotten Son. Amen.

Micah 3:6-10

Grant, Almighty God, that as thou wouldest have us to be ruled by the preaching of thy word, - O grant, that those who have to discharge this office may be really endued with thy celestial power, that they may not attempt any thing of themselves, but with all devotedness spend all their labors for thee and for our benefit, that through them we may be thus edified, so that thou mayest ever dwell among us, and that we through our whole life may become the habitation of thy Majesty, and that finally we may come to thy heavenly sanctuary, where thou daily invites us, as an entrance there has been once for all opened to us by the blood of thy only-begotten Son. Amen.

Micah 3:11 – 4:2

Grant, Almighty God that as thou hast been pleased to erect the throne of thy Son among us, we may rely on his protection and learn to resign ourselves wholly to thee, and never turn aside here and there, but with tulle obedience so submit ourselves to the King who has been appointed by thee, that he may own us as his legitimate people, and so glorify thy name, that we may not at the same time profane it by an ungodly and wicked life, but testify by our works that we are really thy subjects. and that thou attains full authority over us, so that thy name may be sanctified and thy Spirit may really guide us, until at length thy Son, who has gathered us when we were awfully gone astray, gather us again to that kingdom, which he as purchased for us by his own blood. Amen.

Micah 4:3-4

Grant, Almighty God, that since, at the coming of Christ thy Son, thou didst really perform what thy servants, the Prophets, had previously so much foretold, and since thou daily invites us to the unity of faith, that with united efforts we may truly serve thee, - O grant, that we may not continue torn asunder, every one pursuing his own perverse inclinations, at a time when Christ is gathering us to thee; nor let us only profess with the mouth and in words, that we are under thy government, but prove that we thus feel in real sincerity and may we then add to the true and lawful worship of thy name brotherly love towards one another, that with united efforts we may promote each other's good, and that our adoption may thus be proved and be more and more confirmed, that we may ever be able with full confidence to call on thee as our Father through Christ our Lord. Amen.

Micah 4:5-10

Grant, Almighty God, that since under the guidance of thy Son we have been united together in the body of thy Church, which has been so often scattered and torn asunder, - O grant, that we may continue in the unity of faith, and perseveringly fight against all the temptations of this world, and never deviate from the right course, whatever new troubles may daily arise: and though we are exposed to many deaths, let us not yet be seized with fear, such as may extinguish in our hearts every hope; but may we, on the contrary, learn to raise up our eyes and minds, and all our thoughts, to thy great power, by which thou quickenest the dead, and raises from nothing things which are not, so that though we may be daily exposed to ruin, our souls may ever aspire to eternal salvation, until thou at length really slowest thyself to be the fountain of life, when we shall enjoy that endless felicity, which has been obtained for us by the blood of thy only-begotten Son our Lord. Amen.

Micah 4:11 – 5:2

Grant, Almighty God, that as we cease not to provoke thy wrath against us, and as it is needful for us to be often chastised by thy hand, that we may be humbled and learn to submit ourselves to thee in true and willing obedience, - O grant, that we faint not under thy scourges, but ever raise up our minds to the hope of deliverance, which thou givest to us through our Mediator; whom thou hast once for all sent into the world, that thou mightest through him reconcile us to thyself, and through whom also thou bringest help whenever we need it and may we at the same time learn to rely on thy only-begotten Son, so that with courageous minds we may pass through all the miseries of this world, and never at any time grow weary, until having at length obtained the victory, we come to that blessed rest and enjoy the fruit of our victory, through the same Christ our Lord. Amen.

Micah 5:3-6

Grant, Almighty God, that as thou hast from the beginning so defended thy Church, that thou hast never wholly forsaken her, and though it had nearly rejected thee by its defections, yet it has been thy pleasure to stand firm to thy covenant, and to show to it thy favor through all ages, until at length the everlasting Redeemer of the whole world appeared, - O grant, that we may experience the same favor at this day, and though we have in various ways provoked thy wrath against us, yet do thou so humble us, that thou mayest sustain us by thy hand; and may we so recumb on those promises which we find in Scripture, that we may at length by our patience overcome our enemies, and in patience possess our souls, until thou raisest up thine hand, and slowest that invincible power which thou hast given to thy only-begotten Son, that he might repress the devil and all the wicked, and preserve us safe and secure from all injuries. Amen.

Micah 3:7 – 5:15

Grant, Almighty God, that since thou so kindly invites us to thy self, and promises that thy aid should never be wanting to us, provided we do not close the door against thee, - O grant, that though many earthly benefits may be granted to us, we may not yet trust in them and depart from thee, but, on the contrary, recomb on thy grace only: and then should it happen to us to be deprived of all helps, that our minds may be awakened, and that we may thus learn to hasten to thee, may nothing impede our course, that we may not, with the greatest haste and ardent desire, long to deliver up and devote ourselves wholly to thee, that we may be made safe under the care and protection of thy only-begotten Son, whom thou hast appointed to be the guardian of our safety. Amen.

Micah 6:1-8

Grant, Almighty God, that as thou hast made known to us thy Law, and hast also added thy Gospel, in which thou callest us to thy service, and also invites us with all kindness to partake of thy grace, - O Grant, that we may not be deaf, either to thy command or to the promises of thy mercy, but render ourselves in both instances submissive to thee and so learn to devote all our faculties to thee, that we may in truth avow that a rule of a holy and religious life has been delivered to us in thy law, and that we may also firmly adhere to thy promises, lest through any of the allurements of the world, or through the flatteries and crafts of Satan thou shouldest suffer our minds to be drawn away from that love which thou hast once manifested to us in thine only-begotten Son and in which thou daily confirmest us by the teaching of the Gospel, until we at length shall come to the full enjoyment of this love in that celestial inheritance, which has been purchased for us by the blood of thy only Son. Amen.

Micah 6:9-14

Grant, Almighty God, that as thou canst find in us cause enough to execute not only one kind of vengeance, but innumerable kinds of vengeance, so as to destroy us at length altogether, - O grant, that we may of our own accord anticipate thy judgment, and with true humility so abhor ourselves, that there may be kindled in us a genuine desire to seek what is just and right, and thus endeavor to devote ourselves wholly to thee, that we may find thee to be propitious to us: and since we in so many ways offend thee, grant, that in true and sincere faith we may raise up all our thoughts and affections to thy only-begotten Son, who is our propitiation, that thou being appeased, we may lay hold on him, and remain united to him by a sacred bond, until thou at length gatherest us all into that celestial kingdom, which he has procured for us by his own blood. Amen.

Micah 6:15 – 7:4

Grant, Almighty God, that seeing that we are born in a most corrupt age, in which such a license is taken to indulge in wickedness, that hardly a spark of virtue appears, - O grant, that we may yet continue upright in the midst of thorns; and do thou so constantly keep us under the guidance of thy Word, that we may cultivate true piety, and also what is just towards our neighbors: and as there is in us no power to preserve ourselves safe, grant that thy Son may so protect us by the power of the Holy Spirit, that we may continue to advance towards the end of our course, until we be at length gathered into that celestial kingdom, which he has procured for us by his own blood. Amen.

Micah 7:5-10

Grant, Almighty God, that seeing we are at this day surrounded by so many miseries, yea, wherever we turn our eyes, innumerable evils meet us everywhere, which are so many evidences of thy displeasure, - O Grant, that we being truly humbled before thee, may be enabled at the same time to raise up our eyes to the promises of thy free goodness and paternal favor, which thou hast made to us in thine own Son, that we may not doubt, but that thou wilt be propitious to us, inasmuch as thou hast adopted us as thy people: and while our enemies, fully armed, rage and ferociously rise even daily against us, may we not doubt, but that thou wilt be our protection, as thou knowest that we are unjustly troubled by them; and may we thus go on, trusting in thy goodness, seeing that we ever groan under the, burden of our sins, and daily confess that we are worthy of thousand deaths before thee, wert not thou pleased in thine infinite mercy always to receive and restore us to favor, through thy Son our Lord. Amen.

Micah 7:11-14

Grant, Almighty God, that since we have so provoked thy displeasure by our sins, that a dreadful waste and solitude appear everywhere - O Grant, that a proof of that favor, which thou hast so remarkably exhibited towards thy ancient people, may shine upon us, so that thy Church may be raised up in which true religion may flourish, and thy name be glorified: and may we daily solicit thee in our prayers and never doubt, but that under the government of thy Christ, thou canst again gather together the whole world, though it be miserably dispersed, so that we may persevere in this warfare to the end, until we shall at length know that we have not in vain hoped in thee, and that our prayers have not been in vain, when Christ shall exercise the power given to him for our salvation and for that of the whole world. Amen.

Micah 7:15-20

Grant, Almighty God, that as we abound in so many vices, by which we daily provoke thy wrath, and as by the testimony of our consciences, we are justly exposed to everlasting death, yea, and deserve a hundred and even a thousand deaths, - O grant, that we may strive against the unbelief of our flesh, and so embrace thine infinite mercy, that we may not doubt but that thee wilt be propitious to us, and yet not abuse this privilege by taking liberty to sin, but with fear, and true humility, and care, so walk according to thy word, that we may not hesitate daily to flee to thy mercy, that we may thereby be sustained and kept in safety, until having at length put off all vices, and being freed from all sin, we come to thy celestial kingdom, to enjoy the fruit of our faith, even that eternal inheritance which has been obtained for us by the blood of thy only-begotten Son. Amen.

NAHUM

Naham 1:1-5

Grant, Almighty God, that as thou settest before us here as in a mirror how dreadful thy wrath is, we may be humbled before thee, and of our ownselves cast ourselves down, that we may not be laid prostrate by thy awful power, - O grant, that we may by this instruction be really prepared for repentance, and so suppliantly deprecate that punishment which we daily deserve through our transgressions, that in the meantime we may be also transformed into the image of thy Son, and put off all our depraved lusts, and be cleansed from our vices, until we shall at length appear in confidence before thee, and be gathered among thy children, that we may enjoy the eternal inheritance of thy heavenly kingdom, which has been obtained for us by the blood of thy Son. Amen.

Naham 1:6-12

Grant, Almighty God, that inasmuch as thou sees thy enemies at this day raging with cruel, yea, with diabolic fury against thy Church, we may find thee to be the same as the faithful in all former ages had found thee, even a defender of the safety of those who truly, and with a sincere heart, called on thee, and sought thee in extreme necessity; and do thou, at this day, stretch forth thine hand, and so restrain the fury which thou sees is against all thy servants and thy children, that the wicked may at length really find, even to their ruin, that they fight not with miserable mortals, disheartened and without defense, but with thine ineffable power, that they may be confounded, though not ashamed, and that, however they may glamour against thee and thine invincible hand, they may yet become an example and a manifest evidence, that thou art not only faithful in thy promises, but also armed with power, by which thou canst execute whatsoever thou hast promised respecting the preservation of thy Church, until thou at length gatherest us into that blessed rest, which has been provided for us by the blood of thy Son. Amen.

Naham 1:13 – 2:2

Grant Almighty God, that since we are daily chastised by thy scourges, we may know that we are justly punished by thee, and so examine our whole life, that with true and sincere confession we may humbly flee to thy mercy, which is offered to us by thy gospel in Christ our Lord; and since thou dost also show us so many favors, may we not be ungrateful, and may no forgetfulness of thy grace creep over us, but may we especially exercise ourselves through our whole life in the worship of thy name and in giving thanks to thee, and so offer to thee, with our tongues, the sacrifices of praise, that our whole life may be consistent, and thus glorify thy name on earth, that at length we may be gathered into thy celestial kingdom through the same Christ Jesus our Lord. Amen.

Naham 2:3-8

Grant, Almighty God, that as thou constantly remindest us, in thy word, and teachest us by so many examples, that there is nothing permanent in this world, but that the things which seem the firmest tend to ruin, and instantly fall and of themselves vanish away, when by thy breath thou shakest that strength in which men trust, - O grant, that we being really subdued and humbled, may not rely on earthly things, but raise up our hearts and our thoughts to heaven, and there fix the anchor of our hope; and may all our thoughts abide there, and at length, when thou hast led us through our course on earth we shall be gathered into that celestial kingdom, which has been obtained for us by the blood of thy only-begotten Son. Amen.

Naham 2:9 – 3:1

Grant, Almighty God. that as we have now heard of punishments so dreadful denounced on all tyrants and plunderers, this warning may keep us within the limits of justice, so that none of us may abuse our power to oppress the innocent, but, on the contrary, strive to benefit one another, and wholly regulate ourselves according to the rule of equity: and may we hence also receive comfort whenever the ungodly molest and trouble us, and doubt not but that we are under thy protection, and that thou art armed with power sufficient to defend us, so that we may patiently bear injuries, until at length the ripened time shall come for thee to help us, and to put forth thy power for our preservation; nor let us cease to bear our evils with patience, as long as it may be thy will to exercise us in our present warfare, until having gone through all one troubles, we come to that blessed rest which has been provided for us in heaven by Christ Jesus our Lord. Amen.

Naham 3:2-10

Grant, Almighty God, that since by thy awful judgments thou dost show thy displeasure at the pride of this world, we may be ruled by the spirit of meekness, and in such a manner humble ourselves willingly under thy hand, that we may not experience thy dreadful power in our destruction, but being, on the contrary, supported by thy strength, we may keep ourselves in our own proper station and in true simplicity, and, at the same time, relying on thy protection, we may never doubt, but thou wilt sustain us against all the assaults of our enemies, however violent they may be, and thus persevere in the warfare of the cross which thou hast appointed for us, until we be at length gathered into that celestial kingdom, where we shall triumph together with thy Son, when his glory shall shine in us, and all the wicked shall be destroyed. Amen.

Naham 3:11-19

Grant, Almighty God, that as we are not able to keep a firm footing in the way of justice and uprightness, - O grant, that, being governed by thy Spirit, we may restrain ourselves from doing any harm, and thus abstain from all evil deeds, and that we may labor to do good to all, so that we may, by experience, find that all are protected by thee, who so conform themselves to the rule of thy Law, that they take no advantage of the simple, either for the purpose of ruining or of injuring them, but who, being content with their own small portion, know that there is nothing better than to be wholly subject to thee, and to thy guidance: and may we thus live in forbearance and justice towards our neighbors, that we may, at the same time, rely on thy mercy, by which alone we can be defended, and made safe against so many assaults of Satan and of the wicked, until, having at length completed the course of our warfare, we shall come into that blessed rest which has been prepared for us in heaven by Christ Jesus our Lord. Amen.

HABAKKUK

Habakkuk 1:1-6

Grant, Almighty God, that as our sins cry continually to heaven, each of us may turn to repentance, and by condemning ourselves of our own accord may anticipate thy judgment, and thus stir up ourselves to repentance, that being received into favor, we may find thee, whom we have provoked to take vengeance, to be indeed our Father: and may we be so preserved by thee in this world, that having at length put off all our vices, we may attain to that perfection of purity, to which thou invites us; and thus lead us more and more to thyself by thy Spirit, and separate us from the corruptions of this world, that we may glorify thee before men, and be at last made partakers of that celestial glory which has been purchased for us by the blood of thy only begotten Son. Amen.

Habakkuk 1:7-12

Grant, Almighty God, that since thou settest around us so many terrors, we may know that we ought to be roused, and to resist the sloth and tardiness of our flesh, so that thou mayest fortify us by a different confidence: and may we so recumb on thine aid, that we may boldly triumph over our enemies, and never doubt, but that thou wilt at length give us the victory over all the assaults of Satan and of the wicked; and may we also so look to thee, that our faith may wholly rest on that eternal and immutable covenant, which has been confirmed for us by the blood of thy only Son, until we shall at length be united to him who is our head, after having passed through all the miseries of the present life, and having been gathered into that eternal inheritance, which thy Son has purchased for us by his own blood. Amen.

Habakkuk 1:13-17

Grant, Almighty God, that as it cannot be but that, owing to the infirmity of our flesh, we must be shaken and tossed here and there by the many turbulent commotions of this world,-O grant, that our faith may be sustained by this support-that thou art the governor of the world, and that men were not only once created by thee, but are also preserved by thy hand, and that thou art also a just judge, so that we may duly restrain ourselves; and though we must often have to bear many insults, let us yet never fail, until our faith shall become victorious over all trials, and until we, having passed through continued succession of contests, shall at length reach that celestial rest, which Christ thy Son has obtained for us. Amen.

Habakkuk 2:1-3

Grant, Almighty God, that as thou sees us laboring under so much weakness, yea, with our minds so blinded that our faith falters at the smallest perplexities, and almost fails altogether,-O grant that by the power of thy Spirit we may be raised up above this world, and learn more and more to renounce our own counsels, and so to come to thee, that we may stand fixed in our watch tower, ever hoping, through thy power, for whatever thou hast promised to us, though thou shouldst not immediately make it manifest to us that thou hast faithfully spoken; and may we thus give full proof of our faith and patience, and proceed in the course of our warfare, until at length we ascend, above all watch towers, into that blessed rest, where we shall no more watch with an attentive mind, but see, face to face, in thine image, whatever can be wished, and whatever is needful for our perfect happiness, through Christ our Lord. Amen.

Habakkuk 2:4

Grant, Almighty God, that as the corruption of our flesh ever leads us to pride and vain confidence, we may be illuminated by thy word, so as to understand how great and how grievous is our poverty, and be thus taught wholly to deny ourselves, and so to present ourselves naked before thee, that we may not hope for righteousness or for salvation from any other source than from thy mercy alone, nor seek any rest but only in Christ; and may we cleave to thee by the sacred and inviolable bond of faith, that we may boldly despise all those empty boastings by which the ungodly exult over us, and that we may also so cast ourselves down in true humility, that thereby we may be carried upward above all heavens, and become partakers of that eternal life which thine only begotten Son has purchased for us by his own blood. Amen.

Habakkuk 2:5-6

Grant, Almighty God, that as thou deignest so far to condescend as to sustain the care of this life, and to supply us with whatever is needful for our pilgrimage-O grant that we may learn to rely on thee, and so to trust to thy blessing, as to abstain not only from all plunder and other evil deeds, but also from every unlawful coveting; and to continue in thy fear, and so to learn also to bear our poverty on the earth, that being content with those spiritual riches which thou offerest to us in thy gospel, and of which thou makes us now partakers, we may ever cheerfully aspire after that fullness of all blessings which we shall enjoin when at length we shall reach the celestial kingdom, and be perfectly united to thee, through Christ our Lord. Amen.

Habakkuk 2:7-14

Grant, Almighty God, that as we are so inclined to do wrong, that every one is naturally disposed to consider his own private advantage-O grant that we may confine ourselves by that restraint which thou layest on us by thy Prophets, so that we may not allow our coveting to break forth so as to commit wrong or iniquity, but confine ourselves within the limits of what is just, and abstain from what belongs to others: may we also so learn to console ourselves in all our distresses, that though we may be justly oppressed by the wicked, we may yet rely on thy providence and righteous judgement, and patiently wait until thou deliverest us, and makes it manifest that whatever the wicked devise for our ruin, so cleaves to themselves as to return and recoil at length on their own heads; and may we so fight under the banner of the Cross, as to possess our souls in patience, until we at length shall attain that blessed life which is laid up in heaven for us, through our Lord Jesus Christ. Amen.

Habakkuk 2:15-19

Grant, Almighty God, that as there is in us so little of right judgement, and as our minds are blind even at mid-day,-O grant, that thy Spirit may always shine in us, and that being attentive to the light of thy word, we may also keep to the right way through the whole course of our pilgrimage, and subject to thee both ourselves and every action of our life, so that we may not be led by any allurements into the same ruin with the ungodly, who would deceive and entrap us, and who lie in wait on every side; but that being ruled by the counsel of thy Spirit, we may beware of all their intrigues: and may we, especially as to our spiritual life, be so given up to thee alone, as ever to keep ourselves far away from the defilements of all people, and so remain in the pure worship of thy majesty, that the ungodly may never draw us away into the same delusions with themselves, by which Satan so mightily deceives them; but may we follow Him as our leader whom thou wouldst have to be our ruler, even Christ thy Son, until he at length gathers us all into that celestial kingdom which he has purchased for us by his own blood. Amen.

Habakkuk 2:20 – 3:1

Grant, Almighty God, that as thou hast deigned to make thyself known to us by thy word, and as thou elevates us to thyself in a way suitable to the ignorance of our minds,-O grant, that we may not continue fixed in our stupidity, but that we may put off all superstitions, and also renounce all the thoughts of our flesh, and seek thee in the right way; and may we suffer ourselves to be so ruled by thy word, that we may purely and from the heart call upon thee, and so rely on thine infinite power, that we may not fear to despise the whole world, and every adversity on the earth, until, having finished our warfare, we shall at length be gathered into that blessed rest, which thine only-begotten Son has procured for us by his own blood-Amen.

Habakkuk 3:2-7

Grant, Almighty God, that as we have a continual contest with powerful enemies, we may know that we are defended by thine hand, and that even thou art fighting for us when we are at rest; so that we may boldly contend under thy protection, and never be wearied, nor yield to Satan and the wicked, or to any temptations; but firmly proceed in the course of our warfare: and however much thou mayest often humble us, so as to make us to tremble under thine awful judgement, may we yet never cease to entertain firm hope, since thou hast once promised to be to us an eternal Father in thine eternal and only-begotten Son, but being confirmed by the invincible constancy of faith, may we so submit ourselves to thee, as to bear all our afflictions patiently, till thou gatherest us at length into that blessed rest, which has been procured for us by the blood of thine own Son. Amen.

Habakkuk 3:8-13

Grant, Almighty God, that as thou hast so often and in such various ways testified formerly how much care and solicitude thou hast for the salvation of those who rely and call on thee,-O grant, that we at this day may experience the same: and though thy face is justly hid from us, may we yet never hesitate to flee to thee, since thou hast made a covenant through thy Son, which is founded in thine infinite mercy. Grant then, that we, being humbled in true penitence, may so surrender ourselves to thy Son, that we may be led to thee, and find thee to be no less a Father to us than to the faithful of old, as thou everywhere testifies to us in thy word, until at length being freed from all troubles and dangers, we come to that blessed rest which thy Son has purchased for us by his own blood. Amen.

Habakkuk 3:14-19

Grant, Almighty God, that as we cease not daily to provoke thy wrath against us, and as the hardness and obstinacy of our flesh is so great, that it is necessary for us to be in various ways afflicted,-O grant, that we may patiently bear thy chastisements, and under a deep feeling of sorrow flee to thy mercy; and may we in the meantime persevere in the hope of that mercy, which thou hast promised, and which has been once exhibited towards us in Christ, so that we may not depend on the earthly blessings of this perishable life, but relying on thy word may proceed in the course of our calling, until we shall at length be gathered into that blessed rest, which is laid up for us in heaven, through Christ one Lord. Amen.

ZEPHANIAH

Zephaniah 1:1-4

Grant, Almighty God, that as we are so prone to corruptions, and so easily turn from the right course after having commenced it, and so easily degenerate from the truth once known,-O grant, that, being strengthened by thy Spirit, we may persevere to the end in the right way which thou showest to us in thy word, and that we may also labor to restore the many who abandon themselves to various errors; and though we may effect nothing, let us not yet be led away after them, but remain firm in the obedience of faith, until having at length finished all these contests, we shall be gathered into that blessed rest which is prepared for us in heaven, through Christ our Lord. Amen.

Zephaniah 1:5-9

Grant, Almighty God, that as we continue in so many ways to provoke against us thy wrath, we may patiently bear the punishment, by which thou wouldest correct our faults, and also anticipate thy judgment: and since thou art pleased to recall us in due time to thyself, let us not turn deaf ears to thy counsels, but so obey and submit ourselves to thee, that we may become partakers of that mercy, which thou offerest to us, provided we seek to be reconciled to thee, and so proceed in thy service, that under the government of Christ thy Son, whom thou hast appointed to be our supreme and only king, we may so strive to be wholly devoted to thee that thou mayest be glorified through our whole life, until we become at length partakers of that celestial glory, which has been procured for us by the blood of thy only-begotten Son. Amen

Zephaniah 1:10-12

Grant, Almighty God, that as almost the whole world breaks out into such excesses, that there is no moderation, no reason,-O grant, that we may learn not only to confine ourselves within those limits which thou dost approve and command, but also to delight and glory in the smallness of our portion, inasmuch as the wealth, and honors, and pleasures of the world so fascinate the hearts and minds of all, that they elevate themselves into heaven, and carry on war, as it were, avowedly with thee. Grant also to us, that in our limited portion we may be in such a way humbled under thy powerful hand, as never to doubt but that thou wilt be our deliverer even in our greatest miseries; and that ascribing to thee the power over life and death, we may feel fully assured, that whatever afflictions happen to us, proceed from thy just judgment, so that we may be led to repentance, and daily exercise ourselves in it, until we shall at length come to that blessed rest which is laid up for us in heaven, through Christ our Lord. Amen.

Zephaniah 1:13 – 2:2

Grant, Almighty God, that as we continue in various ways to provoke thy wrath, we may at length be awakened by the blasting of that trumpet which sounds in our ears, when thou proclaimest that thou wilt be the judge of the world, and testifies also the same so plainly in the gospel, so that we may, with our minds raised up to thee, learn to renounce all the depraved lusts of the world, and that having shaken off our torpidity, we may so hasten to repent, that we may anticipate thy judgment, and so find that we are reconciled to thee, as to enjoy thy goodness, and ever to retain the taste of it, in order that we may be enabled to renounce all the allurements and pleasures of this world, until we shall at length come to that blessed rest, where we shall be filled with that unspeakable joy, which thou hast promised to us, and which we hope for in Christ our Lord. Amen.

Zephaniah 2:3-8

Grant, Almighty God, that as thou hast been pleased to consecrate us a peculiar people to thyself, we may be mindful of such an invaluable favor, and devote ourselves woody to thee, and so labor to cultivate true sincerity as to bear the marks of thy people and of thy holy Church: and as we are so polluted by so many of the defilements of our own flesh and of this world, grant that thy Holy Spirit may cleanse us more and more every day, until thou bringest us at length to that perfection to which thou invites us by the voice of thy gospel, that we may also enjoy that blessed glory which has been provided for us by the blood of thy only begotten Son. Amen.

Zephaniah 2:9-15

Grant, Almighty God, that as thou triest us in the warfare of the cross, and arouses most powerful enemies, whose barbarity might justly terrify and dishearten us, were we not depending on thine aid,- O grant, that we may call to mind how wonderfully thou didst in former times deliver thy chosen people, and how seasonably thou didst bring them help, when they were oppressed and entirely overwhelmed, so that we may learn at this day to flee to thy protection, and not doubt, but that when thou becomest propitious to us, there is in thee sufficient power to preserve us, and to lay prostrate our enemies, how much soever they may now exult and think to triumph above the heavens, so that they may at length know by experience that they are earthly and frail creatures, whose life and condition is like the mist which soon vanishes: and may we learn to aspire after that blessed eternity, which is laid up for us in heaven by Christ our Lord. Amen.

Zephaniah 3:1-5

Grant, Almighty God, that inasmuch as thou hast deigned to favor us with an honor so invaluable, as to adopt us for a holy people to thee, and to separate us from the world,-O grant, that we may not close our eyes against the light of thy truth, by which thou showest to us the way of salvation; but may we with true docility follow where thou callest us, and never cast away the fear of thy majesty, nor mock thee with frivolous ceremonies, but strive sincerely to devote ourselves wholly to thee, and to cleanse ourselves from all defilements, not only of the flesh, but also of the spirit, that by thus seeking true holiness, we may aspire after and diligently labor for that heavenly perfection, from which we are as yet far distant; and may we in the meantime, relying on the favor of thy only-begotten Son, lean on thy mercy; and while depending on it, may we ever grow up more and more into that true and perfect union, reserved for us in heaven, when we shall be made partakers of thy glory, through Christ our Lord. Amen.

Zephaniah 3:6-9

Grant, Almighty God, that since it is the principal part of our happiness, that in our pilgrimage through this world there is open to us a familiar access to thee by faith,-O grant, that we may be able to come with a pure heart to thy presence: and when our lips are polluted, O purify us by thy Spirit, so that we may not only pray to thee with the mouth, but also prove that we do this sincerely, without any dissimulation, and that we earnestly seek to spend our whole life in glorifying thy name, until being at length gathered into thy celestial kingdom, we may be truly and really united to thee, and be made partakers of that glory, which has been procured for us by the blood of thy only-begotten Son. Amen.

Zephaniah 3:10-13

Grant, Almighty God, that since the depravity of our nature is so great, that we cannot bear prosperity without some wantonness of the flesh immediately raging in us, and without becoming even arrogant against thee,-O grant, that we may profit under the trials of the cross; and when thou have blest us, may we with lowly hearts, renouncing our perverseness, submit ourselves to thee, and not only bear thy yoke submissively, but proceed in this obedience all our life, and so contend against all temptations as never to glory in ourselves, and feel also convinced, that all true and real glory is laid up for us in thee, until we shall enjoy it in thy celestial kingdom, through Christ our Lord. Amen.

Zephaniah 3:14-19

Grant, Almighty God, that as we are at this day so scattered on account of our sins, and even they who seem to be collected in thy name and under thy authority, are yet so torn by mutual discords, that the safety of thy Church hangs as it were on a thread, while in the meantime thine enemies seem with savage cruelty to destroy all those who are thine, and to obliterate thy gospel,-O grant, that we may live in quietness and resignation, hoping in thy promises, so that we may not doubt, but that thou in due time will become our deliverer: and may we so patiently bear to be afflicted and cast down by thee, that we may ever raise up our groans to heaven so as to be heard through the name of thy Son, until being at length freed from every contest, we shall enjoy that blessed rest which is laid up for us in heaven, and which thine only begotten Son has procured for us. Amen.

HAGGAI

Haggai 1:1-4

Grant, Almighty God, that as we must carry on a warfare in this world, and as it is thy will to try us with many contests,-O grant, that we may never faint, however extreme may be the trials which we shall have to endure: and as thou hast favored us with so great an honor as to make us the framers and builders of thy spiritual temple, may every one of us present and consecrate himself wholly to thee: and, inasmuch as each of us has received some peculiar gift, may we strive to employ it in building this temple, so that thou mayest be worshipped among us perpetually; and especially, may each of us offer himself wholly as a spiritual sacrifice to thee, until we shall at length be renewed in thine image, and be received into a full participation of that glory, which has been attained for us by the blood of thy only-begotten Son. Amen.

Haggai 1:5-11

Grant, Almighty God, that since thou kindly and graciously invites us to thyself, we may not wait until thou stimulates us with goads, but cast aside our sloth and run quickly to thee. And when our torpor so possesses us as to render punishment necessary, permit us not to harden ourselves; but being at length effectually warned, and we return to the right way, and strive so to render all we do approved by thee, that we may find a door opened to thy grace and favor: and being made partakers of those blessed, by which thou affordest a taste of that goodness which we shall enjoy in heaven, may we ever aspire thither, and be satisfied with the abundant blessings which we daily and even continually receive from thine hand, in such a manner as not to be detained by this world; but may we, with minds raised up to heaven, ever tend upwards, and labor for that perfect happiness which is there laid up for us by Christ our Lord. Amen.

Haggai 1:12 – 2:5

Grant, Almighty God, that as we are not only alienated in mind from thee, but also often relapse after having been once stirred up by thee, either into perverseness, or into our own vanity, or are led astray by various things, so that nothing is more difficult than to pursue our course until we reach the end of our race,-O grant that we may not confide in our own strength, nor claim for ourselves more than what is right, but, with our hearts raised above, depend on thee alone, and constantly call on thee to supply us with new strength, and so to confirm us that we may persevere to the end in the discharge of our duty, until we shall at length attain the true and perfect form of that temple which thou commandest us to build, in which thy perfect glory shines forth, and into which we are to be transformed by Christ our Lord. Amen.

Haggai 2:6-9

Grant, Almighty God, that since we are by nature extremely prone to superstition, we may carefully consider what is the true and right way of serving thee, such as thou dost desire and approve, even that we offer ourselves spiritually to thee, and seek no other altar but Christ, and relying on no other priest, hope to be acceptable and devoted to thee, that he may imbue us with the Spirit which has been fully poured on him, so that we may from the heart devote ourselves to thee, and thus proceed patiently in our course, that with minds raised upwards we may ever go on towards that glory which is as yet hid under hope, until it shall at length be manifested in due time, when thine only-begotten Son shall appear with the elect angels for our final redemption. Amen.

Haggai 2:10-14

Grant, Almighty God, that inasmuch as we come from our mother's womb wholly impure and polluted, and afterwards continually contract so many new defilements,-O grant that we may flee to the fountain, which alone can cleanse us. And as there is no other way by which we can be cleansed from all the defilements of the flesh, except we be sprinkled by the blood of thy only begotten Son, and that by the hidden power of thy Spirit, and thus renounce all our vices,-O grant that we may so strive truly and sincerely to devote ourselves to thee, as daily to renounce more and more all our evil affections, and to have nothing else as our object, but to submit our minds and all our affections to thee, by really denying ourselves, and to exercise ourselves in this strenuous effort as long as we are in this world, until we attain to that true and perfect purity, which is laid up for us in thine only-begotten Son, when we shall be fully united to him, having been transformed into that glory into which he has been received. Amen.

Haggai 2:15-23

Grant, Almighty God, that as we are still restrained by our earthly cares, and cannot ascend upward to heaven with so much readiness and alacrity as we ought-O grant, that since thou extendest to us daily so liberal a supply for the present life, we may at least learn that thou art our Father, and that we may not at the same time fix our thoughts on these perishable things, but learn to elevate our minds higher, and so make continual advances in thy spiritual service, until at length we come to the full and complete fruition of that blessed and celestial life which thou hast promised to us, and procured for us by the blood of thy only begotten Son. Amen.

ZECHARIAH

Zechariah 1:1-4

Grant, Almighty God, that as thou hast not only once embraced us in thy paternal bosom, when it pleased thee to offer to us the salvation obtained by the death of thine only-begotten Son, but continuest also daily to invite us to thyself, and also to recall the wandering to the right way - O grant, that we may not always remain deaf and hardened against thy warnings, but bring to thee hearts really submissive, and study so to devote ourselves to thee, that it may be evident that we have not received thy grace in vain; and may we also continue in the constant fruition of it, until we shall at length fully attain that blessed glory, which having been obtained for us, id daily set before us by the teaching of the Gospel, that we may be confirmed in it. May we therefore make such continual advances, through the whole course of our life, that having at last put off all the corruptions of our flesh, we may be really united to thee in that perfect purity to which thou invitests us, and which we hope for, through the grace of thine only Son. - Amen.

Zechariah 1:5-11

Grant, Almighty God, that as thou hast not only once embraced us in thy paternal bosom, when it pleased thee to offer to us the salvation obtained by the death of thine only-begotten Son, but continuest also daily to invite us to thyself, and also to recall the wandering to the right way - O grant, that we may not always remain deaf and hardened against thy warnings, but bring to thee hearts really submissive, and study so to devote ourselves to thee, that it may be evident that we have not received thy grace in vain; and may we also continue in the constant fruition of it, until we shall at length fully attain that blessed glory, which having been obtained for us, id daily set before us by the teaching of the Gospel, that we may be confirmed in it. May we therefore make such continual advances, through the whole course of our life, that having at last put off all the corruptions of our flesh, we may be really united to thee in that perfect purity to which thou invitests us, and which we hope for, through the grace of thine only Son. - Amen.

Zechariah 1:12-17

Grant, Almighty God, that though we are continually tossed here and there by various trials, and Satan ceases not to shake our faith, - O grant, that we may yet stand firm on the promise that thou hast once given us, and which thou hast also confirmed through thine only-begotten Son, even that thou wilt ever be propitious and reconcilable to us, so that we may not despair in our greatest troubles, but relying on thy goodness may utter our groans to thee, until the ripened time of our deliverance shall come: nor let us in the meantime envy the evanescent happiness of thy enemies; but patiently wait, while thou showest that the chief object of desire is to have thee propitious to us, and that accursed is every good thing which the ungodly receive while they provoke thee and make thee angry, until Christ shall at length reveal to us the real happiness and glory of thy Church, when he shall appear at the last day for our salvation - Amen.

Zechariah 1:18 – 2:5

Grant, Almighty God, that as we are on every side surrounded by many enemies, and as Satan never ceases to kindle the fury of many, not only to be hostile to us, but also to destroy and consume us, - O grant that we may learn to raise up our eyes to heaven, and trusting in thy protection may boldly fight in patience, until that shall appear which thou hast once testified in this remarkable prophesy, that there are many smiths in thine hall, and many hammers, by which thou breakest in pieces those horns which rise up to scatter us, and until at length, after having overcome all the devices of Satan, we shall reach that blessed rest which has been provided for us by the blood of thine only begotten Son. - Amen.

Zechariah 2:6-10

Grant, Almighty God, that as thou sees that we continually tremble in the midst of dangers, and often stumble and fall through the infirmity of our flesh, - O grant, that we may learn so to rely on the strength and help which thou promisest to us, that we may not hesitate to pass through all kinds of dangers, and boldly and firmly to fight under thy banner; and may we be thus gathered more and more into the unity of thy Church, until having, finished all our troubles and contests, we shall at length reach that blessed and celestial rest which has been obtained for us by the blood of thine only-begotten Son. - Amen.

Zechariah 2:11 – 3:4

Grant, Almighty God, that as thou hast made us a royal priesthood in thy Son, that we may daily offer to thee spiritual sacrifices, and be devoted to thee, both in body and soul, - O grant, that we, being endued with thy power, may boldly fight against Satan, and never doubt but that thou wilt finally give us the victory, though we may have to undergo many troubles and difficulties: and may not the contempt of the world frighten or dishearten us, but may we patiently bear all our reproaches, until thou at length stretches forth thine hand to raise us up to that glory, the perfection of which now appears in our head, and shall at last be clearly seen in all the members, in the whole body, even when he shall come to gather us into that celestial kingdom, which he has purchased for us by his own blood. - Amen.

Zechariah 3:5-9

Grant, Almighty God, that as by nature we do not willingly submit to the reproach and contempt of the world, - O grant, that with our hearts lifted up to heaven, we may become indifferent to all reproaches, and that our faith may not succumb nor vacillate, though profane men may ridicule us while serving thee under the cross: but may we patiently wait, until Christ shall at length appear in the splendor of his priesthood and kingdom; and may we, in the meantime, contemplate the excellency with which thou hast adorned thy Church, and be thus encouraged to connect ourselves with those few and despised men, who faithfully and sincerely follow thy word, and disregard the arrogance of the whole world, and never doubt, but that if we remain grounded in the pure doctrine of the gospel, thou wilt raise us up to heaven, yea, and above all heavens, where we shall enjoy that blessedness which thine only-begotten Son has obtained for us by his own blood. - Amen.

Zechariah 3:10 – 4

Grant, Almighty God, that as thou shinest on us by thy word, and showest to us the way of salvation, we may with open eyes look on that light; and as we are blind also at mid-day, open thou our eyes, and may the inward light of thy Spirit lead us to the light of thy word, that we may not doubt but that thou alone art sufficient to supply us with all those things which are necessary for the enjoyment of celestial life, that by thus distilling on us frequently and continually thou mayest refresh us, so that the light of faith, which has been once kindled in our hearts by thy grace, may never be extinguished, until at length we shall attain to that fullness which has been laid up for us in heaven: and may we thus now in part be satisfied with the measure of knowledge which thou hast given us, until we shall at length see thee face to face, that being thus transformed to thine image, we may enjoy the fullness of that glory into which Christ our Lord has been received. - Amen.

Zechariah 4:7-14

Grant, Almighty God, that since Satan at this day sets against us many terrors to cast us down, and we are very weak, - O grant, that with our eyes lifted above we may meditate on that invincible power which thou possesses, and by which thou canst overcome all the hindrances of this world: and then, when nothing in this world but what is contemptible appears to us as capable to confirm and support our faith, may we, by the eye of faith, behold thine hidden power, and never doubt but that thou wilt at length perform what the world at this day thinks to be impossible and therefore ridicules; and may we so constantly persevere in this confidence, that every one of us may devote to thee his labor to the end, and never faint in the work of promoting the spiritual building, until at length we ourselves shall be gathered, and others shall be gathered through our labors, to offer to thee not only spiritual sacrifices, such as thou receives now from us, but also to offer to thee, together with the angels, eternal sacrifice of praise and triumphant thanksgiving, on seeing perfected what at this day is only weakly begun. - Amen.

Zechariah 5:1-11

Grant, Almighty God, that as thou threatens us with severe punishment to restrain us from sin, we may regard thy judgment, and not abuse thy long-suffering in sparing us for a time; and also that, whenever thou chastises us, we may seriously consider that we deserve thy displeasure, as we have in various ways provoked thy wrath: and may we not at the same time despair or be broken down, but learn so to recomb on thy mercy as not to doubt but that there will be a seasonable end to our evils, and that thou wilt not only mitigate the rigor of punishment as far as necessary for our comfort, but wilt also punish our enemies, so that we may know that nothing is better for us, or more desirable, than to be chastised by thy hand, not that thou mayest destroy us, but recall us to the way of salvation, until we be at length made capable of receiving that favor which has been laid up for us in heaven, through Jesus Christ our Lord. - Amen.

Zechariah 6:1-8

Grant, Almighty God, that since we are here exposed to so many evils, which often suddenly arise like violent tempests, - O grant, that with hearts raised up to heaven, we may acquiesce in thy hidden providence, and be so tossed here and there according to the judgment of our flesh, as yet to remain fixed in this truth, which thou wouldest have us to believe - that all things are governed by thee, and that nothing takes place except through thy will, so that in the greatest confusions we may always clearly see thine hand, and that thy counsel is altogether right, and perfectly and singularly wise and just; and may we ever call upon thee, and flee to this port - that we are tossed here and there, that thou mayest ever sustain us by thine hand, until we shall at length be received into that blessed rest which has been procured for us by the blood of thine only-begotten Son. - Amen.

Zechariah 6:9-15

Grant, Almighty God, that since thy Son has been made known to us, through whom is brought to us the perfection of all blessings and of true and real glory, - O grant, that we may continue settled in him, and never turn here and there, nor fluctuate in any way, but be so satisfied with his kingship and priesthood, as to deliver up ourselves wholly to his care and protection, and never doubt but that we are so sanctified by his grace as to be now acceptable to thee, and that relying on him as our Mediator, we may offer ourselves as a sacrifice to thee with full confidence of heart, and thus strive to glorify thee through the whole course of our life, that we may at length be made partakers of that celestial glory which has been obtained for us by the blood of thy only-begotten Son. - Amen.

Zechariah 7:1-9

Grant, Almighty God, that as we are so inclined to dissimulation, we may learn strictly to examine ourselves, and to descend into our own consciences, so that none of us may sleep in self-delusion, but be so displeased with our hidden vices, as in the meantime to aspire after, and with every care and labor, to attain true religion, and so strive to devote ourselves wholly to thee, that we may groan under the burden of our sins, and so suppliantly flee to thy mercy, as at the same time to be touched with true penitence, until having at length put off the corruptions of our flesh, we shall be received into that purity which has been prepared for us in heaven by Jesus Christ our Lord. - Amen.

Zechariah 7:10-14

Grant, Almighty God, that as thou hast adopted us for this end, that we may show brotherly kindness one towards another, and labor for our mutual benefit, - O grant, that we may prove by the whole tenor of our life, that we have not been called in vain by thee, but that we may so live in harmony with each other, that integrity and innocence may prevail among us; and may we so strive to benefit one another, that thy name may be thus glorified by us; until having at length finished our course, we reach the goal which thou hast set before us, that having at last gone through all the evils of this life, we may come to that blessed rest which has been prepared for us in heaven by Christ our Lord. - Amen

Zechariah 8:1-8

Grant, Almighty God, that though we daily depart from thee by our sins, we may not yet be wholly removed from the foundation on which our salvation depends; but do thou so sustain us, or even raise us up when fallen, that we may ever continue in our degree, and also return to thee in true repentance, and whatever may happen to us, may we learn ever to look to thee, that we may never despair of thy goodness, which thou hast promised to be firm and perpetual, and that especially while relying on thy only-begotten Son our Mediator, we may be able to call on thee as our Father, until we shall at length come to that eternal inheritance, which has been obtained for us by the blood of thine only Son. - Amen.

Zechariah 8:9-13

Grant, Almighty God, that as thou sees us to be cold and frigid, when all our actions ought to be consecrated to thee, and all our members to be devoted to thy service in obedience to thy word, - O grant, that we may every day courageously strive against our natural indifference, and contend with all hindrances, and boldly repel all assaults which Satan may make, so that though our fervor may not be such as it ought to be, we may yet with sincere desire and genuine affection of heart ever advance in the course of our calling, until we reach the goal and be gathered into thy kingdom to enjoy the victory which thou hast promised to us, and with which thou also daily favourest us, until at length it be fully enjoyed, when we shall be gathered into thy celestial kingdom, through Christ our Lord. - Amen.

Zechariah 8:14-19

Grant, Almighty God, that as thou invites us so kindly and graciously to thyself, we may not be refractory, but with every evil affection subdued, offer ourselves to thy service; and since thou requires nothing else from us but to observe what is right towards one another, - O grant that we may be mindful of that brotherhood which thine only-begotten Son has consecrated by his own blood, and call on thee as our Father, and prove by the whole of our conduct that we are thy children; and may every one of us so labor for one another, that being united in heart and affection, we may with one consent aspire after that blessed life, where we shall enjoy that inheritance which has been prepared and obtained by the blood of thy Son, and through him laid up for us in heaven. - Amen.

Zechariah 8:20 – 9:1

Grant, Almighty God, that as thou kindly and graciously extends thy hand to us, not only to show us once for all the right way, but also to lead us through our whole life, and even to sustain us when wearied, and to raise us up when fallen, - O grant, that we may not be ungrateful for this thy great kindness, but render ourselves obedient to thee; and may we not experience the dreadful power of thy judgment, which thou denounces on all thine enemies, who are to sustain a vengeance that is to sink them in the abyss of endless perdition; but may we suffer ourselves to be ever raised up by thy hand, until we shall at length reach that blessed rest, to which thou invites us, and art ready to lead us, where we shall enjoy the fullness of those blessings which have been obtained for us by thy only-begotten Son - Amen.

Zechariah 9:2-8

Grant, Almighty God, that as the ungodly at this day take such delight in their own filth, that the weakness of our faith is somewhat disturbed by their pride and arrogance, - O grant, that we may learn to lift up our eyes to thy judgments, and patiently wait for what is now concealed, until thou puttest forth the power of thine hand and destroyest all those who now cruelly rage and shed innocent blood, and persecute thy Church in every way they can: and may we so cast ourselves on thy care, so as not to doubt but that thou art sufficient for our safety, and that thou wilt at length make evident what thou hast testified, even that there is so much protection in thine hand, as that we may safely boast that we are safe and blessed, as long as thou art pleased to exercise care over us, until we shall at length reach that blessed rest, which has been prepared for us in heaven by Christ our Lord. - Amen.

Zechariah 9:9-12

Grant, Almighty God, that as we do not at this day look for a Redeemer to deliver us from temporal miseries, but only carry on a warfare under the banner of the cross, until he appear to us from heaven to gather us into his blessed kingdom, - O grant, that we may patiently bear all evils and all troubles: and as Christ once for all poured forth the blood of the new and eternal covenant, and gave us a symbol of it in the Holy Supper, may we, confiding in so sacred a seal, never doubt but that he will be always propitious to us, and render manifest to us the fruit of his reconciliation, when after having supported us for a season under the burden of those miseries by which we are now oppressed, thou gatherest us into that blessed and perfect glory, which has been procured for us by the blood of Christ our Lord, and which is daily set before us in the gospel, and laid up for us in heaven, until we at length shall come to enjoy it through the same, our Lord Jesus Christ. - Amen.

Zechariah 9:13-17

Grant, Almighty God, that as we cannot look for temporal or eternal happiness, except through Christ alone, and as thou settest him forth to us as the only true fountain of all blessings, - O grant, that we, being content with the favor offered to us through him, may learn to renounce the whole world, and so strive against all unbelief; that we may not doubt but that thou wilt ever be one kind and gracious Father, and fully supply whatever is necessary for our support. and may we at the same time live soberly and temperately, so that we may not be under the power of earthly things; but with our hearts raised above, aspire after that heavenly bliss to which thou invites us, and to which thou also guides us by such helps as are earthly, so that being really united to our head, we may at length reach that glory which has been procured for us by his blood. - Amen.

Zechariah 10:1-5

Grant, Almighty God, that since constant fightings await us here, and our infirmities are so great that without thy power supporting us we cannot but fall every moment, - O grant, that we may learn to recumb on that help which thou hast promised, and which thou hast also offered to us, and dost daily offer through the Gospel in thine only-begotten Son; and may we distrust our own strength, yea, may we be overwhelmed with despair as to ourselves, not indeed that we may despond, but that we may look upward and seek the aid of thy Spirit, so that we may not doubt but that we shall be equal to our enemies, and even be victorious over them, until having at length finished our warfare, we shall reach that blessed rest which has been obtained for us by the blood of thine only Son. - Amen.

Zechariah 10:6-12

Grant, Almighty God, that as we are constrained continually to groan under the burden of our sins, and the captivity in which we are held justly exposes us to continual trembling and sorrow, - O grant, that the deliverance, already begun, may inspire us with the hope, so as to expect more from thee than what we can see with our eyes; and may we continually call on thee until thou completes what thou hast begun, and puttest to flight both Satan and our sins, so that being in true and full liberty devoted to thee, we may be partakers of that power which has already appeared in our head, until having at length passed through all our contests, we may reach that blessed rest, where we shall enjoy the fruit of our victory in Christ our Lord - Amen

Zechariah 11:1-7

Grant, Almighty God, that as thou hast hitherto so kindly showed thyself to be our Shepherd, and even our Father, and hast carefully provided for our safety, - O grant, that we may not by our ingratitude deprive ourselves of thy favors, so as to provoke thy extreme vengeance, but on the contrary suffer ourselves to be gently ruled by thee, and render thee due obedience: and as thine only-begotten Son has been by thee set over us as our only true Shepherd, may we hear his voice, and willingly obey him, so that we may be able to triumph with thy Prophet, that thy staff is sufficient for us, so as to enable us to walk without fear through the valley of the shadow of death, until we shall at length reach that blessed and eternal rest, which has been obtained for us by the blood of thine only Son. - Amen.

Zechariah 11:8-13

Grant, Almighty God, that as thou ceases not, though provoked by our many sins, to discharge the office of a good and most faithful shepherd, and as thou continues in various ways to testify that Christ watches over us as one who has undertaken the care of our safety, - O grant, that we may be touched with the feeling of true repentance, and so profit under thy scourges, that by considering thy judgments, we may be really humbled under and mighty hand, and so submit to thee, that finding us teachable and obedient, thou mayest continue to rule us to the end, until after having been protected from all harms by the pastoral staff of thine only-begotten Son, we shall at length reach that blessed rest, which has been procured for us by his blood. - Amen.

Zechariah 11:14-17

Grant, Almighty God, that as thou hast hitherto so patiently endured, not only our sloth and folly, but also our ingratitude and perverseness, - O grant, that we may hereafter render ourselves submissive and obedient to thee; and as thou hast been pleased to set over us the best of shepherds, even thine only-begotten Son, cause us willingly to attend to him, and to suffer ourselves to be gently ruled by him; and though thou mayest find in us what may justly provoke thy wrath, yet restrain extreme severity, and so correct what is sinful in us, as to continue to the end our Shepherd, until we shall at length, under thy guidance, reach thy heavenly kingdom; and thus do thou keep us in thy fold and under the guidance of thy pastoral staff, that at length being separated from the goats, we may enjoy that blessed inheritance which has been obtained for us by the blood of thy beloved Son. Amen.

Zechariah 12:1-6

Grant, Almighty God, that inasmuch as the condition of all those who fight under the banner of the cross of Christ seems at this day hard and even miserable, - O grant, that relying on thy promises, by which thou encourages us, we may continually persevere, and not hesitate to remain in thy fold, though wolves lie in wait for us on every side, and robbers also and thieves furiously assail us, so that we may ever remain under the protection of thy hand, and never envy the children of this world on account of their pleasures, ease, and worldly advantages, but patiently bear to be agitated by constant fear, so that we may with quiet minds wait until thou showest to us, when we come to die, that our salvation is safe and secure in thy hand; and having thus at length passed through all troubles, we may come to that blessed rest, which thine only-begotten Son has procured for us by his own blood. - Amen.

Zechariah 12:7-10

Grant, Almighty God, that as we are this day surrounded with enemies, and without any defense, so that our safety seems to be every moment in danger, - O grant, that we may raise up our hearts to thee, and being satisfied with thy protection alone, may we despise whatever Satan and the whole world may threaten us with, and thus continue impregnable while carrying on our warfare, so that we may at length reach that happy rest, where we shall enjoy not only those good things which thou hast promised to us on earth, but also that glorious and triumphant victory which we shall partake of together with our head, even Christ Jesus, as he has overcome the world for us, in order that he might gather us to himself, and make us partakers of his victory and of all his blessings. - Amen.

Zechariah 12:11 – 13:1

Grant, Almighty God, that since thou hast been pleased to adopt us as thy people, and from being thine enemies, profane and reprobate, to make us the children of Abraham, that we might be to thee a holy heritage, - O grant, that through the whole course of our life we may so repent as to attain thy mercy, which is daily set before us in thy gospel, and of which thou hast given us a sure pledge in the death of thy only Son, so that we may become more and more humble before thee, and labor to form our life according to the rule of righteousness, and so loathe ourselves, that we may at the same time be allured by the sweetness of thy goodness to call upon thee, and that being thus united to thee, we may be confirmed in the faith, until we shall reach that blessed rest which has been procured for us by the blood of thy Son Jesus Christ. - Amen.

Zechariah 13:2-5

Grant, Almighty God, that as thou hast been pleased to draw us at this day, by the light of thy gospel, out of that horrible darkness in which we have been miserably immersed, and to render thy face so conspicuous to us in the person of thy only-begotten Son, that nothing but our ingratitude prevents us from being transformed into thy celestial glory, - O grant, that we may make such advances in the light of truth, that every one of us may be ashamed of his former ignorance, and that we may freely and ingenuously confess that we were lost sheep, until we were by thy hand brought back into the way of salvation; and may we thus proceed in the course of our holy vocation, until we shall at length be all gathered into heaven, where not only that truth shall give us light, which now rules us according to the capacity of our flesh, but where also shall shine on us the splendor of thy glory, and shall render us conformable to thine image, through Jesus Christ our Lord. - Amen.

Zechariah 13:6-9

Grant, Almighty God, that as thou sees that we are full of so many sinful desires, which defile whatever purity thou hast conferred on us by thy Spirit, - O grant, that we may daily profit under thy scourges, and so submit ourselves to be ruled by thee, as to become resigned and obedient, even when thou dealest with us with unusual severity; and may we ever taste of the sweetness of thy goodness in thy greatest rigour, and know that thou thereby providest for our safety, and leadest us towards perfect purity, from which we are as yet far distant, so that we may be obedient to thee in this world, and become hereafter partakers of that victory which Christ has procured for us, and enjoy with him his triumph in thy heavenly kingdom. - Amen.

Zechariah 14:1-7

Grant, Almighty God, that since thou hast deigned to separate us to be thy peculiar treasure, and leadest us daily under thy banner, and invites us so kindly and gently by the voice of thy gospel, - O grant, that we may not reject so great a kindness, nor render ourselves unworthy of our holy calling; and whatever evils must be borne by us, may we sustain them with resigned minds, until having at length finished the contests by which thou wouldst now exercise and prove our faith, we shall be received into that blessed rest, which is laid up for us in heaven, and has been purchased for us by the blood of thine only-begotten Son. Amen.

Zechariah 14:8-10

Grant, Almighty God, that as thou gatherest us for this end, that we may be to thee a peculiar people, and as thou hast separated us from profane men, that thy legitimate worship may prevail among us, - O grant, that we may all attend to thy word, and surrender ourselves wholly to thee, and never thorn aside either to the right hand or to the left, but continue to observe the rule which thou hast prescribed, so that we may know by the continual flowing of thy favor that thou rulest in the midst of us; and may we by this enjoyment be stimulated more and more to love, worship, and fear thee, so that consecrating ourselves, body and soul, truly and from the heart, to thee, we may make continual advances in true religion, until having at length put off all the filth of our flesh we shall come to that blessed inheritance, which has been purchased for us by the blood of thy only begotten Son - Amen.

Zechariah 14:11-16

Grant, Almighty God, that as thou sees that thy Church at this day is miserably torn by many discords, and that there are so many traitorous ministers of Satan, who cease not to disturb it, - O grant, that we may find by experience what thou hast promised by thy Prophet, even that thou wilt be the perpetual guardian of those whom thou hast been pleased once to choose as thine own, and whom thou hast received into thine own embrace, so that they may courageously proceed amidst all discords, and come forth at length as conquerors: and may it please thee also to put forth thine hand, and to execute that vengeance which thou hast denounced by the same Prophet, so as to destroy and reduce to nothing not only those who openly oppose thee and thy servants and children, but also those serpents, who by intrigues and frauds and by other base means, harass and torment thy Church, until we shall at length attain a full victory and triumph in thy celestial kingdom, together with our head, even Christ Jesus our Lord. - Amen.

Zechariah 14:17-21

Grant, Almighty God, that as thou hast deigned to choose us as thy peculiar treasure, and to consecrate us to thyself in the person of thy only-begotten Son, - O grant, that we may so follow holiness through the whole course of our life, that thy glory may shine forth in all our works: and may we never undertake anything except for this end - that thy name may be more and more glorified, and may we be holy both in body and soul, and free from all the pollutions of the flesh and of the world, that we may be thus confirmed in the hope of our calling, and be encouraged to proceed during the remainder of our course, until we shall at length reach that glory which has been procured for us by the blood of thine only-begotten Son. - Amen.

MALACHI

Malachi 1:1-5

Grant, Almighty God, that as thou hast not only designed to give us a life in common in this world but hast also separated us from other heathen nations, and illuminated us by the Sun of Righteousness, thine only begotten Son, in order to lead us into the inheritance of eternal salvation, - O grant, that having been rescued from the darkness of death, we may ever attend to that celestial light, by which thou guidest and invitest us to thyself; and may we so walk as the children of light, as never to wander from the course of our holy calling, but to advance in it continually, until we shall at length reach the goal which thou hast set before us, so that having put off all the filth of the flesh, we may be transformed into that ineffable glory, of which we have now the image in thine only-begotten, Son. - Amen.

ALSO

Grant, Almighty God, that as thou best been pleased to adopt us as thy people for this end, that we may be in-grafted as it were into the body of thy Son, and be made conformable to our head, - O grant, that through our whole life we may strive to seal in our hearts the faith of our election, that we may be the more stimulated to render thee true obedience, and that thy glory may also be made known through us; and those whom thou hast chosen together with us may we labor to bring together, that we may unanimously celebrate thee as the Author of our salvation, and so ascribe to thee the glory of thy goodness, that having cast away and renounced all confidence in our own virtue, we may be led to Christ only as the fountain of thy election, in whom also is set before us the certainty of our salvation through thy gospel, until we shall at length be gathered into that eternal glory which He has proctored for us by his own blood. - Amen.

Malachi 1:6-10

Grant, Almighty God, that as thou best been pleased in thine infinite mercy not only to choose from among us some to be priests to thee, but also to consecrate us all to thyself in thine only begotten Son, - O grant, that we at this day may purely and sincerely serve thee, and so strive to devote ourselves wholly to thee, that we may be pure and chaste in mind, soul, and body, and that thy glory may so shine forth in all our performances, that thy worship among us may be holy, and pure, and approved by thee, until we shall at length enjoy that glory to which thou invites us by thy gospel, and which has been obtained for us by the blood of thine only-begotten Son - Amen.

Malachi 1:11-14

Grant, Almighty God, that since thou dost not keep us at this day under the shadows of the law, by which thou didst train up the race of Abraham, but invitest us to a service far more excellent, even to consecrate ourselves, body and soul, as victims to thee, and to offer not only ourselves, but also sacrifices of praise and of prayer, as thou hast consecrated all the duties of religion which thou requirest from us, through Christ thy Son, - O grant, that we may seek true purity, and labor to render, by a real sincerity of heart, our services approved by thee, and so reverently profess and call upon thy name, that really fulfilled in us may that be which thou best declared by thy Prophet - that thy name shall be magnified and celebrated through the whole world, as it was truly made known to us in the person of thine only begotten Son. - Amen.

Malachi 2:1-5

Grant, Almighty God that as thou hast been pleased to choose us at this day thy priests, and hast consecrated us to thyself by the blood of thine only-begotten Son and through the grace of thy Spirit, - O grant, that we may rightly and sincerely perform our duties to thee, and be so devoted to thee that thy name may be really glorified in us; and may we be thus more and more confirmed in the hope of those promises by which thou not only guides us through the course of this earthly life, but also invites us to thy celestial inheritance; and may Christ thy Son so rule in us, that we may ever cleave to our head, and be gathered as his members into a participation of that eternal glory into which he has gone before us. - Amen.

Malachi 2:6-9

Grant, Almighty God, that since thou hast deigned to take us as a priesthood to thyself, and hast chosen us when we were not only of the lowest condition, but even profane and alien to all holiness, and hast consecrated us to thyself by thy Holy Spirit, that we may offer ourselves as holy victims to thee, - O grant, that we may bear in mind our office and our calling, and sincerely devote ourselves to thy service, and so present to thee our efforts and our labors, that thy name may be truly glorified in us, and that it may really appear that we have been in grafted into the body of thy only-begotten Son; and as he is the chief and the only true and perpetual priest, may we become partakers of that priesthood with which thou hast been pleased to honor him, so that he may take us as associates to himself; and may thus thy name be perpetually glorified by the whole body as well as by the head. - Amen.

Malachi 2:10-12

Grant, Almighty God, that as we are so inclined to all kinds of wickedness, we may learn to confine ourselves within the limits of thy word, and thus restrain all the desires of our flesh; and that whatever Satan may contrive to draw us here and there, may we continually proceed in obedience to thy word, and being mindful of that eternal election, by which thou hast been pleased gratuitously to adopt us, and also of that calling by which thy eternal election has been confirmed, and by which thou hast received us in thine only-begotten Son, may we go on in our course to the end, and so cleave, by persevering faith, to Christ thy Son, that we may at length be gathered into the enjoyment of that eternal kingdom which he has purchased for us by his blood. - Amen.

Malachi 2:13-16

Grant, Almighty God, that though we daily in various ways violate the covenant which thou hast been pleased to make with us in thine only-begotten Son, we may not yet be dealt with according to what our defection, yea, the many defections by which we daily provoke thy wrath against us, do fully deserve; but suffer and bear with us kindly, and at the same time strengthen us that we may persevere in the truth and perform to the end the pledge we have given to thee, and which thou midst require from us in our baptism, and that we may each of us so conduct ourselves towards our brethren, and husbands towards their wives, that we may cherish that unity of spirit which thou hast consecrated between us by the blood of thine own Son. - Amen.

Malachi 2:17 – 3:3

Grant, Almighty God, that since we are by nature so prone to rash judgement, we may learn to submit to thee, and so quietly to acquiesce in thy judgements, that we may patiently bear whatever chastisements thou mayest daily allot to us, and not doubt but that all is done for our well-being, and never murmur against thee, but give thee the glory in all our adversities; and may we so labor to mortify our flesh, that by denying ourselves we may ever allow thee to be the only true God, and a just avenger, and our Father, and that thus renouncing ourselves, we may yet never depart from the purity of thy word, and be thus retained under thy yoke, until we shall at length attain that liberty which has been procured for us by thine only-begotten Son. - Amen.

Malachi 3:4-8

Grant, Almighty God, that since thou hast been pleased to choose us as priests to thyself, not that we may offer beasts to thee, but consecrate to thee ourselves, and all that we have, - O grant, that we may with an readiness strive to depart from every kind of uncleanness, and to purify ourselves from all defilements, so that we may duly perform the sacred office of priesthood, and thus conduct ourselves towards thee with chasteness and purity; may we also abstain from every evil work, from all fraud and all cruelty towards our brethren, and so to deal with one another as to prove through our whole life that thou art really our Father, ruling us by thy Spirit, and that true and holy brotherhood exists between us; and may we live justly towards one another, so as to render to each his own right, and thus show that we are members of thy only-begotten Son, so as to be owned by him when he shall appear for the redemption of his people, and shell gather us into his celestial kingdom. - Amen.

Malachi 3:9-14

Grant, Almighty God, that since we continue to afford many and various reasons to induce thee to withdraw thy blessing, and to show thyself displeased with us, - O grant, that we may patiently bear thy scourges, by which thou chastises us, and also profit under them, and so contend with all our depraved affections and the corruptions of the flesh, that we may become partakers of thy paternal kindness, which thou offerest to us, and also so taste of thy goodness, which in innumerable ways is manifested towards us, that it may keep us in the pursuit of true religion; finally, may our tongues be consecrated to magnify thy judgement and to celebrate thy justice, that whatever happens to us, we may always serve thee through our whole life as our Father, and declare also thy goodness towards us, and confess that we are justly punished whenever thou visitest us with severity, until we shall at length reach that blessed rest, which is to be the end of all our evils, and an entrance, not only into life, but also into that full glory and happiness, which has been procured for us by the blood of thine only-begotten Son. - Amen.

Malachi 3:15-17

Grant, Almighty God, that as Satan strives to draw us away from every attention to true religion, when things in the world are in a state of disorder and confusion, - O grant, that we may know that thou caress for us; and if we perceive not this by what we find in the world, may we rely on thy word, and doubt not but that thou ever watches over our safety; and being supported by this confidence, may we ever go on in the course of our calling: and as thou hast deigned to make us partakers of that evidence of thy favor, by which we know that we are reconciled to thee in thine only-begotten Son; and being thus made his members, may we never hesitate cheerfully to offer to thee our services, however defective they may he, since thou hast once promised to be a propitious Father to us, so as not rigidly to try what we offer to thee, but so graciously to accept it, that we may know that not only our sins, which justly deserve condemnation, are forgiven and remitted to us, but that thou also so bearest with our infirmities and our defects in our imperfect works, that we shall at length receive the reward which thou hast promised, and which we cannot attain through our merits, but through the sanctification of thy Spirit, and through the sprinkling of the blood of our Lord Jesus Christ. - Amen.

Malachi 3:18 – 4:2

Grant, Almighty God, that as thou hast appointed thine only-begotten

Son to be like a sun to us, we may not be blind, so as not to see his brightness; and that since he is pleased to guide us daily into the way of salvation, may we follow him and never be detained by any of the impediments of this world, so as not to pursue after that celestial life to which thou invitest us; and that as thou hast promised that he is to come and gather us into the eternal inheritance, may we not in the meantime grow wanton, but on the contrary watch with diligence and be ever attentively looking for him; and my we not reject the favor which thou hast been pleased to offer us in him, and thus grow torpid in our dregs, but on the contrary be stimulated to fear thy none and truly to worship thee, until we shall at length obtain the fruit of our faith and piety, when he shall appear again for our final redemption, even that sun which has already appeared to us, in order that we might not remain involved in darkness, but hold on our way in the midst of darkness, even the way which leads us to heaven. - Amen.

Malachi 4:3-6

Grant, Almighty God, that as nothing is omitted by thee to help us onward in the course of our faith, and as our sloth is such that we hardly advance one step though stimulated by thee, - O grant, that we may strive to profit more by the various helps which thou hast provided for us, so that the Law, the Prophets, the voice of John the Baptist, and especially the doctrine of thine only-begotten Son, may more fully awaken us, that we may not only hasten to him, but also proceed constantly in our course, and persevere in it until we shall at length obtain the victory and the crown of our calling, as thou hast promised an eternal inheritance in heaven to all who faint not but wait for the coming of the great Redeemer. - Amen.

Printed in Great Britain
by Amazon